Women Enter the Wilderness

By Donald J. Greiner

The Notebook of Stephen Crane (editor)

Comic Terror:
  The Novels of John Hawkes

Robert Frost:
  The Poet and His Critics

American Poets Since World War II:
  Ammons through Kumin (editor)

American Poets Since World War II:
  Levertov through Zukofsky (editor)

The Other John Updike:
  Poems/Short Stories/Prose/Play

John Updike's Novels

Adultery in the American Novel:
  Updike, James, Hawthorne

Understanding John Hawkes

Domestic Particulars:
  The Novels of Frederick Busch

Women Enter the Wilderness:
  Male Bonding and the American Novel of the 1980s

Women
Enter
the
Wilderness

Male Bonding and
the American Novel of the 1980s

DONALD J. GREINER

University of South Carolina Press

Copyright © 1991 by the University of South Carolina

Published in Columbia, South Carolina, by the University of South Carolina Press

Manufactured in the United States of America

Library of Congress Cataloging-in-Publication Data

Greiner, Donald J.
  Women enter the wilderness : male bonding and the American novel
of the 1980s / Donald J. Greiner.
      p.   cm.
  Includes bibliographical references (p.   ) and index.
  ISBN 0-87249-749-6 (hardback : acid-free).—ISBN 0-87249-776-3
(pbk. : acid-free)
  1. American fiction—20th century—History and criticism.
2. Masculinity (Psychology) in literature.   3. Wilderness areas in
literature.   4. Friendship in literature.   5. Sex role in
literature.   6. Women in literature.   7. Men in literature.
I. Title.
PS374.M37G74   1991
813'.5409353—dc20   91-6891

For Ellen,
as always, and for
Katherine Murphy Greiner, RN
and
Daniel James Greiner, MD,
lifegivers

Contents

Acknowledgments

Acknowledgments are always a pleasure to write. Professor Joel Myerson, former Chair of the Department of English at the University of South Carolina, helped in numerous ways. The University of South Carolina provided much-needed released time through the granting of a sabbatical. Carol Cutsinger typed the entire manuscript. My graduate assistant Susan Kennedy checked primary sources with accuracy and good humor. Two of my most helpful and supportive colleagues, Professors Ina Hark and Benjamin Franklin V, read parts of the manuscript and suggested revisions. My greatest debts are to my good colleague in contemporary American literature, Professor David Cowart, for reading the entire manuscript and for debating the issues with grace and intelligence; and to Professor Sue Rosser, Director of Women's Studies at the University of South Carolina, for reading parts of the manuscript, for lending books and essays, and for joining me at lunch to discuss ideas. I am out on a limb with this book, but these and other colleagues have helped me hold on.

Don Greiner
July 1990

Women Enter the Wilderness

Introduction

" 'Always give your main character a best friend,'
and he meant a guy."

—*Jesse Hill Ford to Ben Greer*
when the latter was beginning his career;
as told by Mr. Greer to Don Greiner.

My goals in this book are modest. A study of ten American novelists of the 1980s from the contrasting theoretical perspectives of traditional literary criticism on the one hand and of contemporary biodeterminist and feminist anthropology on the other, *Women Enter the Wilderness* is not a theory of American literature or a manual on how to read the American novel. It is, however, an analysis of some unexpected new directions in recent American fiction and of whether these changes do or do not illustrate prevailing theoretical accounts of how the literary canon is defined. For the most part the writers discussed in the following pages are not yet the subjects of extended critical examination. They are Frederick Busch, John Irving, Larry Woiwode, Ben Greer, Richard Russo, Padgett Powell, Robert B. Parker, E. L. Doctorow, Marianne Wiggins, and Gloria Naylor. "Opening up the canon" is a catch-phrase in current literary discourse and a project that I support, but it is not the primary purpose of this book.

By "prevailing theoretical accounts," I mean not the opinion that values Nathaniel Hawthorne more than Susan Warner but the paradigm of traditional American fiction that shows males abandoning the hearth for the wilderness in order to bond while pursuing an elusive freedom that translates into an avoidance of women. One thinks immediately of *The Last of the Mohicans*, *Moby-Dick*, and *Adventures of Huckleberry Finn*—classic novels, novels of male privilege, and novels that have formed the basis of such influential and long-lasting theories as those by D. H. Lawrence, R. W. B. Lewis, and Leslie Fiedler. In these canonical fictions and the theories formulated around them, men in search of what Lewis calls *space* are recalled by women to the test of time. Women represent domesticity, society, and finally mortality; but men desire freedom, wilderness, and most of all immortality. Novels deemed worthy of canonization, novels from Cooper through Hemingway and the Faulkner of *Go Down, Moses* to Saul Bellow and the James Dickey of *Deliverance*, are written by white males and illustrate the paradigm as defined by Lawrence, Lewis, and Fiedler. I have no quarrel with the classic status of these writers, nor do I dismiss the theoretical accounts that have canonized them. Males do bond in canonical American fiction, they do plunge into the territory, and they do try to escape females. In the following chapters, however, I argue that novels written by white males in the 1980s accept the first two parts of the paradigm—men bonding and then escaping to the wilderness—but reject the third—women left behind. The question is why.

To suggest answers I discuss in the first chapter the theories of American literature as advanced by Lawrence, Lewis, Fiedler, and Joel Porte. Because their ideas are familiar to many but not to all, I examine their comments primarily in the context of *The Last of the Mohicans* because I find Cooper's tale of Natty and Chingachgook and of Cora and Alice to be the most influential rendering in American literature of bonded males crossing the border to escape women and the limitations of time. Carolyn Heilbrun calls such canonical fiction "the masculine wilderness of the American novel," and I shall keep her observation in mind as well as those from other of her essays as I offer a reading of Dickey's *Deliverance* to suggest Cooper's long legacy in the novel of masculine prerogative.

The remaining sections of *Women Enter the Wilderness* discuss matters new to the study of traditional and contemporary American fiction. For rather than merely observe that Natty-Chingachgook, Ishmael-Queequeg, Huck-Jim, and their more recent followers bond, I investigate the rationale behind the bonding. To do so, I turn in the second chapter to anthropology, especially the biodeterminist anthropology of Lionel Tiger and Robin Fox. To the disapproval of feminist anthropologists but with the support of such sociobiologists as E. O. Wilson, Tiger and Fox argue the primacy of male bonding as the central force in human evolution. Their theories of man-the-hunter stress the importance of the male and illustrate from the perspective of social science several reasons for the oddly skewed gender relationships in the canonical novel. To balance Fiedler's suggestions of latent homoeroticism in the fictions of male bonding, I also discuss in chapter 2 Eve Kosofsky Sedgwick's remarks on homosocial vs. homoerotic relationships and Heilbrun's comments on androgyny. As in chapter 1, Cooper's fiction, particularly *Mohicans* and *The Prairie*, is my touchstone for traditional American literature.

In the third chapter I examine the now simmering but about-to-boil-over controversy between Tiger's biodeterminist theories of men in groups and the rebuttal by such feminist scholars and anthropologists as Ruth Bleier, Sally Slocum, and Donna Haraway.[1] This examination is central to my general point because I find that novels written by white males in the 1980s extend the biodeterminist-canonical novelist position on male bonding in the wilderness but reject the exclusion of women. The males in novels by Busch, Irving, Woiwode, and Russo bond as they leave the stability of the home for an adventure in the territory, but unlike their precursors in *Mohicans*, *Huckleberry Finn*, or *Deliverance*, they take the female with them or find her already there. This is an astonishing change in the gender relationships of the American novel and one that has occurred as the ideas of feminist scholars in general and feminist anthropologists in particular have helped redirect the artistic consciousness of the culture.

As a relevant sidelight one might consider the contrast between the portrayal of gender in recent American films and its counterpart in contemporary American novels. In *From Reverence to Rape: The Treatment of Women in the Movies*, Molly Haskell argues that "backbiting jealousy, cattiness, and triviality" are invariably characteristics assigned to female roles, the very qualities that "real" men seek to avoid when they leave home.[2] Such buddy films as *Easy Rider* and *Scarecrow* that depict the longing for an "all-male world" are part of the covert backlash against the gains of the women's movement, while films by Stanley Kubrick and Sam Peckinpah are overtly misogynist. The results, says Haskell, are the substitution of violence and sex for romance, and the declining need in movies for "exciting and interesting women" (323–24). Haskell pulls no punches when describing the parts mistakenly accepted by the public as "great women's roles" in the films of the 1960s and 1970s: "Whores, quasi-whores, jilted mistresses, emotional cripples, drunks. Daffy ingenues, Lolitas, kooks, sex-starved spinsters, psychotics. Icebergs, zombies, and ballbreakers" (327–28). The film protagonist who is sensitive, or alienated, or baffled, or idealistic, or triumphant is invariably male. More important, perhaps, is that the directors are also invariably male.

The novels of the 1980s examined here offer a portrayal of gender relationships different from those in movies. Written by white males and investigating male bonding, these fictions nevertheless recognize, accept, and celebrate the importance of women. Thus in chapter 4 I discuss variations on the paradigm of canonical American fiction as seen in Busch's *Sometimes I Live in the Country*, Irving's *A Prayer for Owen Meany*, Woiwode's *Born Brothers*, Greer's *The Loss of Heaven*, Russo's *The Risk Pool*, Powell's *Edisto*, and Parker's *A Catskill Eagle*. In each discussion I suggest intertextual affinities between the contemporary novelists and the canonical writers they acknowledge—primarily Cooper, Hawthorne, Melville, and Twain—in order to show the continuity of the tradition even while I argue that the more recent authors consciously modify it. The inclusion of Robert Parker, a detective writer, might seem curious, but I want to illustrate that the revision of the paradigm affects some modes of popular fiction as well. The hard-boiled detective novel is traditionally a bastion of male privilege and female denigration, and the detective is nearly always a loner. Thus it is significant that Parker, the heir of Dashiell Hammett and Raymond Chandler, bonds his sleuth to a black man and then stresses their bonding to a woman. The final novel discussed in chapter 4 is Doctorow's *Billy Bathgate*. To include it in this section is risky because, although *Billy Bathgate* shows two men bonding and taking a female with them into the wilderness, Doctorow's novel remains traditional in terms of gender relationships. The woman is not an equal partner or a source of strength but a commodity and an object of exchange. By discussing *Billy Bathgate*, I concede what the reader already suspects: that not every important novel written by a white male in the 1980s contributes to the reconsideration of the paradigm that is the center of this study.

The final chapter is not a conclusion but a coda. Rather than summarize what has already been said, I speculate about the parallel matter of female bonding in order to suggest additional areas of investigation. Biodeterminists argue that females do not bond. Feminist anthropologists disagree. Thus I consider two novels of female bonding written by women in the 1980s, Wiggins's *John Dollar* and Naylor's *The Women of Brewster Place*. My context is the anthropological-sociological research by Sarah Blaffer Hrdy and Carol B. Stack: *The Woman That Never Evolved* and *All Our Kin: Strategies for Survival in a Black Community*. The wildernesses in these novels are an island (Wiggins) and a ghetto (Naylor). Like the males in books by Busch and Irving, the females bond to cross the border to the territory, but unlike the gender relationships in *Sometimes I Live in the Country* and *A Prayer for Owen Meany,* Wiggins's and Naylor's women generally do not value men or include them in order to guarantee the bond. Why this should be so is the subject for additional study, but the issue of bonding in contemporary fiction by female writers provides an appropriate coda to *Women Enter the Wilderness: Male Bonding and the American Novel of the 1980s.*

Notes

1. For an overview of the impact of feminist anthropology, see Louise Lamphere, "The Struggle to Reshape Our Thinking about Gender," *The Impact of Feminist Research in the Academy,* ed. Christie Farnham (Bloomington: Indiana University Press, 1987) 11–33.

2. Molly Haskell, *From Reverence to Rape: The Treatment of Women in the Movies* (Baltimore: Penguin, 1974) 248.

Chapter One

Male Bonding and Literary Theory:
The Examples of Cooper and Dickey

Years ago, when I finally left the various schools where I had studied James Fenimore Cooper, Nathanial Hawthorne, Herman Melville, and Mark Twain—but not Harriet Beecher Stowe, Kate Chopin, or Mary E. Wilkins Freeman—I chanced on an essay by Carolyn Heilbrun. Titled "The Masculine Wilderness of the American Novel," the article was ostensibly a commentary on James Dickey's *Deliverance* (1970).[1] Reading Heilbrun's remarks, however, I learned that her broader subject was the prevailing definition of the American novel, a definition that ignored women as both subject matter and writer. Generally unknown today, her short essay is in one sense a starting point for the analysis in the following pages, and thus I should like to note some of the highlights of her argument.

Describing *Deliverance* as the "apotheosis of manliness" for American fiction, she defines the classic American novel—the novel that I was taught and that shapes the foundation of many influential theories of American fiction—as itself the territory where "women do not go, where civilization cannot reach, where men hunt one another like animals and hunt animals for sport" (41). For Heilbrun, *Deliverance* is a highly readable version of what Leslie Fiedler discusses in *Love and Death in the American Novel* (1960) as fiction that insists on the separation of men from women, or on what Heilbrun calls "the woman-despising American dream." Dickey's innovation of men raping each other, says Heilbrun, may be shocking, but it is no more than what the novel of the masculine wilderness has been preparing for since the early nineteenth century.

Although Heilbrun goes on to discuss Dickey and Charles Dickens as different novelists with the similar effect of denying total humanity to women, her primary point is that both novelists are typical of male writers in general for being "profoundly anti-androgynous" (41). The irony is that authors who avoid androgyny often lock both male and female readers into a prison of gender. I will have more to say later about Heilbrun's explanation of androgyny, but for the moment I am interested in her thesis that American novelists and American critics deny humanity to half the race. Arguing that, except for American fiction, the novel in general is the one literary form that has expressed the "hidden, denied, and civilizing androgynous impulse," Heilbrun names *The Scarlet Letter* (1850) as the only classic American novel that resists the fantasy of two or more men fleeing women to find freedom from domesticity in the tangled but liberating domain of the American wilderness.

My point is that novels reflect culture, and culture in America means separation of male and female. The separation was particularly acute in the nineteenth century, so much so that century-old definitions of gender continue to direct contemporary notions of the sexes. As Heilbrun notes in another essay, "More and more as I study the post-Victorian period, it becomes clear to me how fatally disparate the sexes were allowed to become in the middle years of the nineteenth century. No age has so violently wrenched apart the feminine and masculine impulses of humanity, nor so disastrously named them and confined them to gender."[2] Yet, insists Heilbrun, the novel in general celebrates women characters. One thinks immediately of Henry James, Thackeray, Flaubert, Hawthorne, and Richardson; not to mention Jane Austen, George Eliot, Edith Wharton, and the Brontës. Outside the United States, outside what F. Scott Fitzgerald memorably described in a metaphor of maternity as the "fresh, green breast of the new world," the novel has characterized women as either the bearers or sharers of the moral burden, and it has done so by simultaneously accepting androgyny and rejecting the manly virtues of the curious American fantasy that privileges masculine aggression in a territory promising limitless possibility because it refuses entry to the women who might tame it. Thus, says Heilbrun in a direct challenge to the standard critics of American fiction, most American novels are outside the mainstream of the genre because they turn away from fully drawn women.

Unlike Heilbrun, I do not focus on the place of American fiction in the long history of the genre, but I am concerned with the development of the American novel and with some of its changes in the 1980s. Heilbrun's provocative remarks are all the more stimulating when read in the context of the theories of American fiction that have directed readers, critics, and, one suspects, writers for nearly half a century.

I

Specialists in American literature can readily name the scholars and their books which have had an influence of such enormous range that even today the critic who would question their assumptions must propose countertheories against them. One has in mind such studies as F. O. Matthiessen's *American Renaissance: Art and Expression in the Age of Emerson and Whitman* (1941), Lionel Trilling's *The Liberal Imagination* (1950), Charles Feidelson, Jr.'s *Symbolism and American Literature* (1953), and Richard Chase's *The American Novel and Its Tradition* (1957). But not all serious readers of American literature are specialists, and thus I comment on the positions of four other critics whose theories are not only as stimulating as these but also so influential that they have both shaped an entire culture's understanding of American fiction and defined the place of the novel in American society. The four critics are D. H. Lawrence, R. W. B. Lewis, Leslie Fiedler, and Joel Porte. The paradigm they offer has nevertheless become controversial because of their attitudes toward gender. The issue of gender and its effect on male bonding in the American novel, especially the contemporary novel, is my primary concern. Rather than gloss entire theoretical arguments, however, I shall focus on the critics' analyses of *The Last of the Mohicans* (1826), as well as offer my own commentary on and interpretation of Cooper, because I find *Mohicans* to be, despite its stylistic infelicities, the archetypal tale of male bonding in American literature. In addition, a new reading of *Deliverance* as a contemporary re-creation of Cooper will illustrate its startling affinities with the novel of the nineteenth century.

My purpose is not to rehash familiar material but to use the material to note an unfamiliar change. For while it is clear that the theories I examine have long directed discussions of American fiction until the fairly recent revaluations by feminists, Marxists, and deconstructionists, it is not so evident that many contemporary American writers have assimilated the classic American novel as written by Cooper, Melville, and Twain, and yet have adjusted the prevailing definitions of the novel as argued by Lawrence, Lewis, and Fiedler. Unlike Russell J. Reising, who generally disapproves of every critic mentioned here because of what he sees as exclusivity and political naïveté, I find that their theories continue to exert positive influence, but with this crucial and necessary development: Frederick Busch, Larry Woiwode, John Irving, and others adapt the tradition rather than copy it.[3] These writers experienced their undergraduate years in the 1950s and 1960s when the arguments of Lewis and Fiedler shaped evaluations of the canon, and many of them continued their associations with universities in the 1980s when challenges to the theories became acute. One thinks, for example, of Busch and Colgate University, of Woiwode and SUNY-Binghamton.

Reading this short list of contemporary novelists, one might ex-claim, *Whose* American novel? Such a protest would be based on the observation that the writers named are all white, middle-class males. But that is just the point. The American novel that has come to be known as classic, that has dominated the literary canon, and that has inspired the notions of culture which Lawrence and Lewis defined, was written by white, middle-class males. While one regrets exclusiv-ity, one cannot ignore the effects of literary history—however dis-torted—on succeeding literary generations. What concerns me in the following chapters is not the necessity of opening up the canon (a project that I very much support) but the need of examining how representative male novelists in the late twentieth century have read-justed materials shaped by classic male novelists in the mid nine-teenth century.

D. H. Lawrence was among the first critics to designate these earlier writers as classic, and he did so in a book noted for its idio-syncrasy as well as its influence. Published in 1923 and thus before the rediscovery of Poe, Cooper, and Melville in the twentieth cen-tury, Lawrence's *Studies in Classic American Literature* purported to de-liver the truth to an American reading public that, Lawrence claimed, longed for the safety of "double meaning" when it refused to accept explicitness in its literature.[4] One of Lawrence's truths—and it is a truth that has been expanded by later theorists of American fiction—is that the first Americans crossed the Atlantic not to find freedom but to get away from themselves. Lured by the promise to be "mas-terless," which Lawrence defines negatively as "a hopeless sort of constraint," these Americans confused freedom with escapism be-cause they never decided what they "positively wanted to be" (14). Although Lawrence does not specify the distinction, one understands that he is talking about males when he discusses the American need to shake off control of any sort. Always implied but never developed is the hint that females personify the constraint from which males would escape.

Reading the opening chapter of *Studies in Classic American Liter-ature*, one realizes how the notion of the *masculine* wilderness of the American novel took shape. Yet Lawrence is critical of the national need to flee, of the cultural mandate to pull up stakes and head west whenever the first sign of control impedes freedom. He points to a hidden irony in the classic American novel, that men are free only when they belong to what he calls a "living, organic, *believing* com-munity" which, one assumes, includes women (17). If Lawrence's paradox is accurate, if it is true that males are liberated only when

they belong, then he indirectly describes the pathos of Natty
Bumppo and Chingachgook, who pursue freedom by plunging deeper
into the forest, always headed west. Contrary to one's understanding
of Natty (and of Ishmael and Huck and even Hester), Lawrence argues that the most "unfree souls" go west, and as they do, they
shout of freedom. His general point is that the definition of freedom
depends on the recognition of home. Although he does not say so,
one senses that home means community and that community means
the kitchen, the nursery, the bedroom; in short, women. Thus one is
free—paradoxically—when one abandons the "illusion of doing what
one likes" (17). Only then will the new whole man be realized.

The first significant attempt at such realization, though not in
Lawrence's terms, was Cooper's Leatherstocking saga. Despite
Lawrence's proclaimed "love" of the series, he reads the books as
chronicling not genuine freedom but "wish-fulfilment." Longing,
like many Americans, to escape home, wife, and self, Cooper in-
vented wigwam, Chingachgook, and Natty. The invention is not so
strange because men (but not women, one presumes) live by "lies."
What Lawrence saw, and what subsequently became significant for
Melville and Ishmael, Twain and Huck, Hemingway and Nick Adams, and Bellow and Augie March, is that the first odd couple in
American fiction, the first bonded duo lighting out for the territory to
escape the inhibition of home, was not Natty and Chingachgook but
Natty and Cooper. Wife meant reality, but Natty meant freedom.
Thus when Mrs. Cooper spoke of "the coarser and more revolting,
though more common points" of life, Cooper deflected the mundane
by conjuring up his wish for an Apollo in the guise of a Mohican (58).
Anticipating Fiedler's *Love and Death in the American Novel* by almost
forty years, Lawrence perceived the homosocial (as opposed to homosexual) bond between the ideal hunter and the ideal Indian when
Chingachgook assumes the role of Cooper's substitute wife. The first
masculine wilderness of the American novel is for Lawrence "a sort
of American Odyssey" with Natty as Odysseus (59). Bumppo indeed
has mythic status in the national culture, but one must point out that
the American Ulysses does not return home.

Nor does he want to. Natty's perpetual plunge beyond the border may be an illusion of freedom as defined by Lawrence, but it is
nevertheless clear that Cooper longs to exchange the male-female
constraint for the male-male bond. The former signifies stability in
the bedroom, but the latter promises Eden without the snake. That
Cooper assigns to his Native American Apollo the nickname of the
Great Serpent is an irony he may not have intended, but the fact

remains that the male bond in the form of brotherhood between two races was Cooper's means of escaping the reality of the male-female relationship. Stressing the illusion of Cooper's dream of endless male companionship, Lawrence correctly notes that the white author would never have endured extended proximity to the red chief. A man of society but a dreamer of myth, Cooper needed the regularity of civilization, personified in his wife, in order to create the freedom of legend. The new Eden of the masculine wilderness is a domain without sex, and thus it is clear even to Cooper that the pristine, bonded males cannot perpetuate themselves. Lawrence theorizes that Cooper dreamed "beyond democracy" and that the immaculate friendship of Natty and Chingachgook promised a society even better than that of the emerging United States. Such a society would be based on the "new human relationship" of bonds deeper than fatherhood, marriage, or love, and its nucleus would always be two men.

But where Lawrence sees in Cooper a myth of youth reborn as the premise of America, I find a womanless sphere of perpetual possibility in the Leatherstocking series. Women represent the old, the stable, the present. The theme of men without women gains ascendancy in American literature with the mythologizing of Natty Bumppo and Chingachgook despite Cooper's understanding that civilization in the guise of women always prevails. The issue for the bonded males is not only sexlessness but freedom. And yet as Lawrence shrewdly observes, Cooper could not voice his vision until he was "crystallised in society and sheltering behind the safe pillar of Mrs. Cooper" (66). One senses that dreams need the ordinariness of the real before they metamorphose into myth. Similarly, men need the stability of women before they search out freedom with other men. Suspecting that the presence of women means the absence of myth, Cooper has it both ways: he sends his womanless males into the territory of everlasting possibility, but he himself remains behind with a woman to give a framework to his dream.

When women do leave the parlor for the forest, as in *The Last of the Mohicans,* disaster strikes with such force that both the surrogate son of Natty and the surrogate wife of Natty and Chingachgook must die. Uncas and Cora represent the best that two different civilizations have to offer, but male-female bonding is out of place in the new Eden. Integrity of soul depends on avoidance of flesh. Thus when Lawrence identifies the essential American with the famous description of "hard, isolate, stoic, and a killer," he means—though he does not say so—not women but men, and not red men but white (73). Defining what he calls the "collapse of the white psyche," he concludes by observing that the white male is always divided between "innocence and lust" (72). To escape the stigma of sex, men must avoid the women of society. Other writers, in later novels, question the promise of male bonding. In *Moby-Dick*, for example, Ishmael must abandon his symbolic soulmate Queequeg so as not to contaminate the integrity of the chase in the purity of the ocean. Melville's masculine wilderness finally prohibits the male bond as vehemently as the female presence, and thus one is not surprised that as classic American literature developed in Whitman's "Song of Myself," the journey of the questing male is only that of the self, alone.

Thirty years after Lawrence's seminal study, R. W. B. Lewis published *The American Adam: Innocence, Tragedy, and Tradition in the Nineteenth Century*.[5] Like Lawrence, whom he acknowledges, Lewis is interested in a "native American mythology." But his discussion of male bonding in the masculine wilderness differs from Lawrence's because he is concerned with why a "sense of promise and possibility" no longer dominates American literature. One knows from reading Lewis's prologue that he has only men in mind and that the portrayal of males in the literature of the nineteenth century has defined American culture in the twentieth century: "A century ago, the image contrived to embody the most fruitful contemporary ideas was that of the authentic American as a figure of heroic innocence and vast potentialities, poised at the start of a new history" (1). Aware that the image was illusory, but intrigued by its potency, Lewis indirectly personifies the image of man without woman when he identifies it as Adam before the Fall. Sprung from nowhere, "emancipated" from history, "undefiled" by family, and standing alone, the hero in American fiction—nearly always male—casts off the "usual" inheritances and plunges into the experience of the endless wilderness. That he is undefiled because free of the traditional encumbrances of wife and family is a given.

The hero as Adam begins in the American novel with Natty Bumppo. Although the later protagonists of Hawthorne and Melville suffer the tragic consequences of their own innocence, the male bonding of Dimmesdale-Chillingworth and of Ishmael-Queequeg has its germ in Natty-Chingachgook. All this seems obvious today, but what Lewis brings to the analysis of American culture is the notion of the hero's position in space and time. Noting that American novelists posit their Adam figures outside time so that their "location is essentially in space alone," Lewis defines their habitat as spaciousness: "the unbounded, the area of total possibility" (91). Although Lewis, like Lawrence, focuses primarily on *The Deerslayer* (1841), one thinks immediately of Natty's first appearance in *The Prairie* (1827):

> The whole party was brought to a halt, by a spectacle as sudden as it was unexpected. The sun had fallen below the crest of the nearest wave of the Prairie, leaving the usual rich and glowing train on its track. In the centre of this flood of fiery light a human form appeared. . . . The figure was colossal; the attitude musing and melancholy. . . . The effect of such a spectacle was instantaneous and powerful. The man in front of the emigrants came to a stand, and remained gazing at the mysterious object, with a dull interest, that soon quickened into superstitious awe.[6]

Natty seems to emerge from the sun itself, out of nowhere, standing alone in the endless space of the American prairie, a figure of reverence and religious speculation—until both emigrants and readers realize that time has taken its toll, that the Adam figure before them is an old, old man.

What Heilbrun calls the masculine wilderness, Lewis calls space. Although an unconscious bias toward male experience surfaces when he praises Cooper for taking the Adamic figure "out of the cities and cellars and putting him where he belonged"—in the forest or the prairie, or on the sea—Lewis is surely correct in naming Cooper as the author who brings the American literary hero fully to life by equating his longing for boundlessness with the "area of possibility" (98, 99). Cities and cellars mean domesticity and women. Worse, although Lewis does not say so, domesticity and women mean time. Time is always the enemy of spaciousness for the bonded male in the American novel because, if possible immortality is associated with space, certain mortality is equated with time. Women mean expulsion from the garden and the ticking of the clock. If men are to fulfill the destiny of America—and it is clear in the classic American novel that women cannot do so—then they must avoid the reality of time for the illusion of space. Women in American fiction are nearly always identified with the domestic, and the domestic is invariably tied to social forms. Cooper's one great contribution was to pit individual conduct (read male) against social mandate (read female). Lewis even suggests that the friction between solitary man and domestic responsibilities is the primary measure of American culture: "possibly the one gift indispensable to the narrative artist who aspires to transmute American experience into story: the gift for seeing life dramatically as the measurement by conduct of institutions and the measurement by institutions of conduct" (100). This is why, in Lewis's understanding of the Adamic hero, the Natty Bumppo figure must find his role outside society. For Cooper, the solitary male with his bonded companion and the social hierarchy with its regulatory need must always "appraise each other" (101).

But reading the American novel of the 1980s, one wonders about the male experience in the wilderness if the individual begins inside the social contract. If he is not born purely in space, and if he is always already aware of time, can he survive when he and his companion cross the border and enter the trees? Cooper knows, of course, that Natty and Chingachgook must die, so he works backward from their old age in *The Pioneers* (1823) to their immaculate youth in *The Deerslayer* and thereby guarantees their immortality in myth. Yet while he was consciously creating a myth of male bonding, he was also unconsciously shaping a fantasy of culture. Evidence of the power of the fantasy is the number of twentieth-century novelists adapting the nineteenth-century vision. Lewis is probably correct when he observes that Cooper "felt the myth at a greater depth than did most of his trend-following" contemporaries; and that the more Cooper lost faith in history, the more he sought refuge in art (103). By the publication of *The Scarlet Letter*, a quarter century after *Mohicans* but a scant nine years after *Deerslayer*, the tension between the Adamic male companions and the society that gives them definition by contrast turns toward tragedy.

Lewis concludes with a little-remembered epilogue of four pages which he titles "Adam as Hero in the Age of Containment." Assessing what was for him the contemporary novel of the 1920s–50s, he points to twentieth-century skepticism of the Adamic adventure in the territory beyond the threshold. Aware that the new hopelessness is as "simpleminded" as the old innocence, he criticizes novelists and readers for dismissing the possibility of myth in favor of the burden of history. He finds two serious consequences of the rejection of hope in the modern American novel: antagonism to nature and distrust of experience. Lewis does not name the novels of pessimistic vision that he has in mind. I find, however, that the fiction of Frederick Busch, Richard Russo, John Irving, Larry Woiwode, and others, while not a reprise of Cooper's Edenic hope in *The Last of the Mohicans* and *The Deerslayer*, is nevertheless a celebration of experience in a nature necessarily diminished. Similarly, the "odd aura of moral priority" that Lewis notices in the modern novels he does name and approve—J. D. Salinger's *The Catcher in the Rye* (1951), Ralph Ellison's *Invisible Man* (1952), and Saul Bellow's *The Adventures of Augie March*

(1953)—is less of a factor in American writing of the 1980s, if by moral priority one means Cooper's myth of perpetual possibility. The ghosts of Natty and Chingachgook remain a felt presence in contemporary fiction, and the male bond is as significant to American culture as ever, but with this unexpected difference: women now belong in the forest.

With more exuberance than Lewis, Leslie Fiedler probes the centrality of the American paradigm of men without women. Indeed, in *Love and Death in the American Novel* he names in his preface the very writer whom Lewis praises in his epilogue: Saul Bellow.[7] Rather than locate Augie March in the tradition of Natty Bumppo, however, Fiedler finds a "homoerotic" *Tarzan of the Apes* in Bellow's *Henderson the Rain King* (1959). Fiedler's reference has merit—it is surely no joke—but as one concedes its validity, one points out that while Henderson and Romilayu (not to mention Henderson and Dahfu) are bonded males in the tradition of Natty and his Indians, the bonding does not hold. Dahfu dies, Romilayu is left behind, and Henderson flees the wilderness of Africa for the domesticity of Lily, that is, a woman. Henderson's repudiation of what he calls "unreality" and his acceptance of a reality that always ends in death signal that his sleep is burst and that he must return to, as it were, the settlement where women uphold the rules.

Still, like R. W. B. Lewis before him (who is not mentioned), Fiedler acknowledges the impact of Lawrence's *Studies in Classic American Literature*. Naming Lawrence as the critic who is "closest to the truth" about American novels, Fiedler finds in his predecessor confirmation of the "duplicity and outrageousness" that determine the quality of classic American literature (xiii). But he differs markedly from the commentators who wrote before him. Rather than stress the Adamic potential of male bonding in the new Eden of the American wilderness, he argues that "images of the savage and the colored man" have been established since the time of Charles Brockden Brown as "threats to stable and organized life." One thinks of Chingachgook, Hard Heart, Queequeg, Jim, Sam Fathers, and Romilayu, but where one sees bonded brothers, Fiedler finds the unconscious, "the darker impulses of the id" (148). And more: instead of reading the forest as the limitless domain of infinite potential, or of space, or even of the masculine wilderness of the American novel, he argues that American writers use the forest as another projection of the unconscious.

One recognizes the innovation of Fiedler's reading of Cooper. Describing Cooper as a "businessman writing for other businessmen

and their wives," he stresses that the creator of Natty and Chingachgook did not believe his own myth, and that Cooper did not hesitate
to publish fairy tales of flight from domestic comfort to male companionship beyond the border because he was convinced that no one
would believe him (153). Natty and Chingachgook, then, are no
more than Cooper's idealized projections of resentment against his
comfortable life in a feminized society that he clearly desired and
would always defend.

Safe in his study and close to his wife, Cooper created a bour-
geois image of man-the-hunter as hero and then paired him with an
Indian who typifies "forbidden impulses" in the dreams of the civilized readership. Fiedler's claims for Cooper are large: "His primi-
tives resemble more closely than the wild clansmen of Scott the
version of the Noble Savage proposed by the rudimentary anthropology of the Encylopedists and used by them as controls against which
the corruption and effeminacy of the civilized European could be defined" (170). Lamenting the paucity of mythic material in the United
States, as did Hawthorne and James later, Cooper could lay the
groundwork for subsequent analyses of American culture because he
located his bonded men on the border between society and the wilderness and then immortalized them with the pathos of a lost cause.

For all the sensationalism of his thesis that miscegenation is the
secret theme of *The Last of the Mohicans*, Fiedler's general argument is
more important: that *Mohicans*, like *Robinson Crusoe*, *Ivanhoe*, and
Treasure Island, is a boy's book, a male fantasy which encourages a
flight out of the drawing room, away from mothers and wives, but
with another male of a different race or class. For Fiedler, "the pure
anti-female romance" is "the central myth of our culture," and thus
to identify *Mohicans* as a boy's book is not to denigrate it but to
understand its expression of "the most deeply underlying image of
ourselves" (175).

One of my points, which I will develop later, is that in much
contemporary American fiction "the pure anti-female romance" of
men without women is no longer an inviting fantasy with its attendant reverberations, but for the moment it is important to remember
that not mimesis but myth was the issue for Cooper. Although he
created in his fiction the illusion of the need to break from apron
strings and skirts, he accepted in his daily life the sentimental notion
of the sanctity of women. Fiedler is blunt: Cooper's "dream of an
idyllic union with the red man was his inner escape from a world of
blameless, sexless females. Only the Indian in him, which is to say
the unconscious, is allowed to blaspheme against the pale-face vir-

gin" (179). Fiedler's opinion is a long way from the purity of Lewis's American Adam, and it seems likely that the fantasy of a bonding among a few immaculate men can hold firm only so long as writers persuade themselves and their readers to project the illusion onto the literary hero.

Such projection seems impossible today, but it is a truth of American literary history that Cooper created a paradigm for subsequent novelists whether they read him or not. When Fiedler describes the Leatherstocking tales as "the world's first Westerns," he calls attention to the tenacity of a national art form. While Natty Bumppo as the isolated hunter and Chingachgook as the noble chief are separate myths, the two join to shape the enduring third myth of men of different circumstances bound not to society but to nature and each other. What interests Fiedler, and what I believe stands in the background of a contemporary re-creation of the myth such as James Dickey's *Deliverance*, is that for all the idealization of Natty, the hunter remains "a dangerous symbol" of the novelist's revolt against the inhibitions of home and women. Although Leatherstocking refuses to kill man or beast unless he has to, he becomes a figure of anarchy in the American imagination because he and his companion define the law of the moment. When the regulations that control civilized discourse in the women-dominated space of the kitchen and parlor fit too tightly, the anxious American male heads for the territory where the law is what he says it is or, better, where there is no law and surely no woman.

Anxiety thus prompts the myth of male bonding. Whether Chingachgook represents what Fiedler says Cooper "had stifled to be worthy of his wife and daughters," or whether the innocent brotherhood of males was an effort to exorcise fear of an Indian uprising, the masculine retreat to the wilderness is not always innocent (190). The irony is that terror and death lurk in the heart of the unfettered territory despite the efforts by male novelists to depict the space beyond the border as beneficent and pure. In *The Last of the Mohicans*, then, Cooper asks the complicated question: What happens when women enter the forest? The answer is increased violence and, worse, a confusing of the "moral priority" that Lewis discusses.

That Cooper first brought to the American novel the model of the erotic brunette and the pure blonde is now an accepted fact, but Fiedler also argues that this pattern became "the standard form in which American writers project their ambivalence toward women" (197). While the plot of *Mohicans* is an escape from the real to the dream—from the home to the forest—the theme is a serious consideration of the havoc wrought by women and by Cooper's "nightmare" of miscegenation. *Mohicans* may ignore history even as it purports to illustrate it, but the fact remains that Magua and Uncas may not marry Cora, and that Natty and Chingachgook may not have any woman at all. The latter two are the heroes who do not get the girl, not because they lack genital masculinity, but because their masculinity is defined by myth. Contemporary male American novelists often have it both ways, joining masculine flight to the wilderness and sexual consummation with women. For Cooper and many subsequent writers, however, the ideal of male bonding opposed the reality of female companionship. If American novelists vest moral authority and its related inhibitions in women—and one thinks of Alice Munro, Phoebe Pyncheon, Miss Watson, Addie Bundren, and Ma Joad— then marriage to the female means diminishment of the male. The ideal of male bonding is tarnished in any other location except the forest. Fiedler is quite insistent: "The very end of the pure love of male for male is to *outwit* woman, that is, to keep her from trapping the male through marriage into civilization and Christianity" (210). Most readers readily accept the innocence of the bonding because they understand that to light out for the territory is to quest for Eden.

Citing Lawrence, Lewis, and Fiedler, Joel Porte, the final critic I discuss here, revises Fiedler's analysis of Cooper's portrayal of women.[8] Acknowledging the paradox that in fleeing the authority of the father in old Europe, the American male novelist faced the tyranny of the mother in new America, Porte argues that Natty Bumppo avoids not "carnality per se, but rather the awful implications of mixing good and evil (religion and sex, as it were) as they are represented by the confusing single image of woman" (10). Moral simplicity, not sexual purity, is the issue. Carrying the heavy burden of natural goodness, Natty must prohibit the entry of corrupt civilization into the wilderness. To establish virtue is to abandon women.

Borrowing from Melville, Porte's fortunate phrase for the masculine wilderness of the American novel is "a paradise for bachelors." For Porte, Cooper's treatment of women surrounding bonded males is more than the establishing of blonde and brunette archetypes; it is a means of investigating the myth of the American Adam. Not miscegenation but a Miltonic equation of sex with the Fall is the foundation for the bonded males' repudiation of women. Idealizing the New World as a new beginning, Cooper accepted an older myth that dramatized how sexuality in the guise of the feminine precipitates confusion, loss, and death. The appearance of Alice and Cora in the forest causes the murder of Uncas, the best man though stained by and punished for his desire of Cora, and prompts Cooper's re-vision of the biblical expulsion from the garden. Paradise is possible only when bachelors rule the territory.

Marriage or even sexual encounter would raise the specter of moral ambiguity in the bonded males and thereby hasten their fall from the mythic to the mundane. Cooper does not suggest that women in the forest are evil. The evil is the side effect of their tempting the male hero away from his moral priority. To accommodate women is to concede one's sexuality; to concede sexuality is to acknowledge one's humanity; to acknowledge humanity is to accept one's death. Porte writes, "One might say that Natty revenges himself on female sexuality by insisting on treating women unsexually" (27). This is why Chingachgook, though bonded to Leatherstocking, can never be his equal. The Indian chief is always the father of Uncas. Both men combine what Porte calls "prelapsarian virtue with postlapsarian knowledge," and thus both understand the paradox when they unite commitment to moral rigor and skill with the gun and the bow.

One wonders how conscious Cooper was of the irony. Did he realize that in naming Chingachgook the "Big Sarpent" after the archetypal snake which, as Natty says, "outwitted" the first woman, he was encouraging Leatherstocking to invite the new serpent into the new Eden? If so, then he implied through metaphor that the ideal domain of the masculine wilderness would always give way to the encroaching society of the female household. Cooper chooses the Big Sarpent rather than Eve so that together Natty and Chingachgook can avoid the gender which, in Miltonic myth, was weak enough to cause the Fall. The implication seems clear: Given the choice between the devil or domesticity, the bonded American male will choose the devil.

Natty's death in *The Prairie*, then, may be attributed to the invasion of spaciousness by the power of time, but it may also be assigned to what Porte sees as "the shift from a patriarchal to a matriarchal society" (47). In the course of *The Prairie*, Esther tames Ishmael Bush, Ellen Wade tames Paul, and Inez tames Middleton. Matriarchy is cited as a means of joining Old World culture with New. But despite Porte's legitimate observation, one understands that matriarchy assumes power only in the settlement. At the conclusion of *The Prairie*, Natty will face the sun to die, but the three couples must turn toward society to live. In the nineteenth-century novel the masculine wilderness can never accommodate women. Even more puzzling is

that at the end of *The Prairie* the wilderness seems also to have expelled men. Leaving a dying Natty at the far reaches of the west, the
couples return east to where they belong. One finally wonders
whether Natty must die *because* women reestablish the power of the
marriage bond.

II

The narrator and hero of James Dickey's heart-thumping *Deliverance* is already married.[9] This one fact with its accompanying obligation to sustained sexual activity forever separates mundane Ed
Gentry from mythic Natty Bumppo. Dickey's masculine wilderness
waits to be delivered, while Cooper always hopes that his is pristine.
Just as the loss of cultural aspiration means the diminishment of the
American hero for Cooper, so the waste of territory itself—what
R. W. B. Lewis called space—means for Dickey a similar though culturally less devastating shrinking. Natty and Chingachgook inch
westward in an effort to maintain Eden. Ed and Lewis Medlock
hurry to the Cahulawassee River in an effort to beat the real estate
developers. Dickey's bonded males, as well as those of other contemporary novelists, fall short of Natty and Chingachgook not because
they are more realistically imagined but because the national culture
will no longer sustain the illusion of the ideal.

Dickey's apotheosis of the theme of manliness in American fiction re-creates *The Last of the Mohicans*. Whether Dickey was conscious of the reference is beside the point. One agrees with Fiedler
that Cooper's mythic adventure intuitively excites the imagination of
the American male. In this sense, then, *Deliverance* looks to the past
of the American novel. Not only are women prohibited from crossing
the clearing to enter the woods, but Lewis, the contemporary rein-
carnation of Natty Bumppo, is embarrassed by a male camaraderie
that indulges in sexual innuendo. Ed, for example, can describe his
current work in advertising as "Take some photographs for Kitts Tex-
tile Mills. Kitt'n Britches. Cute girl in our britches stroking her
pussy. A real cat, you understand." Lewis, however, is uneasy with
such talk: " 'Too bad,' Lewis said, and grinned, although talk about
sex was never something he seemed to enjoy" (8). Dickey's intertextual irony is that the Leatherstocking figure can no longer be the
focus of the tale. Natty can avoid sex, kill Indians, and describe the
mythic and cultural implications of his experience beyond society.
Lewis may match Natty on the first two counts, but Ed Gentry assumes the other third of Leatherstocking's characterization. Sex is
not to be avoided, though women must always stay at home.

Dickey divides the archetypal male of American fiction because the culture no longer supports the burden of a mythic hero. His bonded males must rely on each other, but they are always aware of their differences. Escaping from the limitation of time to the freedom of space, and from the circumscription of society to the openness of the woods, Natty believes in eternal possibility despite the sound of the axes behind him. He does not find the immortal in life, but he does achieve it in myth. He and Chingachgook are together forever in the forest. Dickey's irony is that Ed can play Chingachgook to Lewis's Natty except that in the diminished culture of the late twentieth century Ed must distance himself from the hero. The bonding holds firm, but the specter of doubt has entered the forest. Lewis has a face like a hawk, and he realizes that his enemy is time, but Ed understands how Lewis stands apart from both Natty and himself: "But Lewis and I were different, and were different from each other. I had nothing like his drive, or his obsessions. Lewis wanted to be immortal. He had everything that life could give, and he couldn't make it work. . . . He was the kind of man who tries by any means—weight lifting, diet, exercise, self-help manuals from taxidermy to modern art—to hold on to his body and mind and improve them, to rise above time" (9). Natty hears the sound of axes and moves farther west toward a still-available Eden. Lewis hears, on the other hand, the engines of bulldozers felling trees and damning rivers, and he needs to touch base again with the wild paradise of nature before he returns to time and the city, the only place left for him to go.

To flee time is to avoid women. Ed does not share his companion's compulsion. He believes, of course, that women are a menace in the forest, but as a man of the settlement, he accepts the limitation of sexuality. One assumes that Chingachgook does too, or at least that he did so at one time, for he is the father of Uncas. But with Mohican women no longer available, and with Cooper's insistence on racial purity as his guide, the Big Sarpent abstains from sexual encounters. It is almost as if Cooper transfers his suspicion of racial mixing to a prohibition on gender mixing, all in the service of myth.

Dickey, however, substitutes male fantasy for heroic myth. Although he banishes women from the wilderness as fervently as Cooper, his narrator's attitude is much more sexist than Leatherstocking's. Ed's sense of women is not necessarily a character flaw, but he clearly lacks Natty's tone of nostalgia and regret that women cannot peacefully enter the forest without tainting the prospect for Eden.

Yet if Dickey keeps women physically out of the wilderness, he allows their indirect presence via dreams. The gender issue from the male perspective is explicit, and this is where Dickey creates the apotheosis of Cooper's paradigm. For Ed's witticism about the model and her pussycat is no joke. Male bonding may encourage sexually charged wisecracks about women, but Dickey's larger point is that Ed turns a silly jest into a male fantasy that is sexist and yet has the strength to offer a promise.

Just before he plunges into the male wilderness, Ed recalls the female model. He assumes, however wrongly, that in her eyes partial nudity merely goes with the job, and from his point of view her apparent nonchalance triggers a dream that sustains him throughout his ordeal:

> She turned and looked into my face at close range, and the gold-glowing mote fastened on me; it was more gold than any real gold could possibly be; it was alive, and it saw me. Standing this close, she changed completely; she looked like someone who had come to womanhood in less than a minute. . . . She simply took her left breast in her hand, and the sight of that went through me, a deep and complex male thrill (22).

With that male thrill Dickey unites Alice Munro's golden blondeness with Cora's invitation to passion, and his bonded male exchanges the reality of femininity for the promise of fantasy. As Ed has sex with his wife immediately before joining Lewis for the escape from women, he remembers the vision in the dream rather than the woman in the bed: "The girl from the studio threw back her hair and clasped her breast, and in the center of Martha's heaving and expertly working back, the gold eye shone, not with the practicality of sex . . . but the promise of it that promised other things, another life, deliverance" (28). Like Cooper, Dickey bars women from the wilderness and thus extends the male bias of the classic American novel. But unlike his predecessor, he carries the fantasy of ideal sex into the woods—"not with the practicality of sex . . . but with the promise of it that promised other things"—and thereby indulges the male dream of the erotic as transformation of the mundane. His irony, and it is a stunning twist to the canonical American novel of male bonding, is that sex without women lurks around the bend once men leave the settlement for the forest. Ed's illusion of the promise of "other things" generated by the model's mysterious golden eye turns into the ultimate nightmare of male companionship: men sexually violating other men.

The sexless marriage of innocent, heroic men imagined by Cooper becomes perverted in the late twentieth century when novelists re-create the paradigm. This is because the masculine wilderness no longer nurtures intimations of an ideal domain. Dickey's extension and then reversal of Cooper speak to gender issues that have charged the American novel since the 1960s: where Cooper maintained the purity of the forest by prohibiting women, Dickey excludes the very women who might cleanse the territory soiled by masculine violence. Lawrence's description of "hard, isolate, stoic, and a killer" applies primarily to those pristine, mythic men who kept to themselves, observed their moral code, and shot to kill when necessary. When Dickey implicitly assigns the same adjectives to both the bonded males and the bad Indians—the Georgia mountain men who attack Ed and Lewis—he illustrates how far the traditional cultural ideal has degenerated. If Ed Gentry is to survive once Lewis is injured, he must do more than kill animals for food. He must become the beast himself. The Big Sarpent assumes command when Natty Bumppo falls by the wayside. Flushed with the sexual fantasy of the model's naked breast and golden eye, he retaliates against males who sexually pollute the purity that the wilderness is supposed to represent. In doing so, he soils his own soul.

Bowing to Chingachgook, Ed must become the snake. When *Deliverance* was published, Dickey remarked, "I'm tired of reading novels in which nothing happens. Books like that are really rehearsals for some imagined literary display" (*Time* 20 April 1970). His comment unintentionally directed readers to the scenes in which things happen: the homosexual rape, the murders by bow and arrow, the long climb up the cliff. But supporting these actions is the complexity of animal-like savagery. Dickey exposes what Cooper conceals: that each male harbors an unknown part of the self that he fears to face because he might have to acknowledge his own intrinsic beast. Worse, forced into a disaster on the far side of sanctioned sex in the bedroom and the regulations of the daily routine, the bonded males must not only recognize but also cultivate their bestial instincts. In short, they must slither with the snake.

Cooper's interest in the founding of a civilization becomes in Dickey a concern with how to save it. His irony is that survival depends on the ability to shed the inhibitions of civilization and to call forth the monster, to meet the buried self face to face, and to revert willingly to an animal brutality once thought mastered. With Lewis Medlock, the Leatherstocking figure in quest of immortality, unexpectedly incapable of leadership because of an injury that negates his longing to personify the Cooper myth, Ed must first locate the level of the beast and then persuade himself to kill. For Dickey, moral priority gives way to the stronger instinct of survival. Bashed by the Cahulawassee River and threatened by an unknown assailant who rapes and murders, Ed flounders out of the moral equation that Dickey identifies with the promise of deliverance by the woman with the golden eye.

In Dickey's re-reading of *The Last of the Mohicans*, Lewis (Natty), Bobby (David Gamut), and Drew (Uncas) are not as important as Ed primarily because the novel chronicles the latter's search for what he calls "harmony": "I liked harmoniousness and a situation where the elements didn't fight with each other or overwhelm each other" (19). A harmony that he can accommodate is indulging his erotic fantasy of the model while having sex with his wife. As opposed to Lewis's belief in madness, Ed seeks to live by "sliding," by meeting life's little hurdles in a gentlemanly, nonviolent manner. He is in every way a man of the town, but the nightmare in the big woods teaches him that he must become a beast in the forest. Thus it is significant that at the beginning of his flight from women to the company of men he senses a dimension within himself just the other side of wakefulness that he longs to reach but cannot define. All he can do is generalize it as "a point, a line or border": "There was something about me that usually kept me from dreaming, or maybe kept me from remembering what I had dreamed; I was either awake or dead, and I always came back slowly. . . . Something in the world had to pull me back, for every night I went down deep, and if I had any sensation during sleep, it was of going deeper and deeper, trying to reach a point, a line or border" (25).

Dickey clarifies the connection between Ed's experience while sleeping and his trek down the river when, on first feeling the urgency of the current, Ed remembers the "moment of losing consciousness at night, going toward something unknown that I *could not avoid*, but from which I would return" (73, my emphasis). Only in the wilderness does he take the initial step toward defining the border that Natty can always avoid by moving westward. Aware that he is now in an unexplored land where creatures with one forepaw lifted surround him, Ed witnesses what Melville, writing of Hawthorne, called "the blackness of darkness." He does not yet understand what he is seeing, and he surely does not believe that one of the creatures with forepaw lifted is a man. But once he identifies during his first night in the forest with something undeniably wild—the owl on his tent—he begins the process of recognizing his bestiality.

Cooper need not consider such extreme measures because, as he conceives of Leatherstocking, Natty is always sure of his humanity, of his status as a man without a cross. Dickey, however, cannot assume such certainty in a shrunken culture of diminished myth. Thus he shows Ed questioning his humanity during the moral dilemma that follows the rape of Bobby and the murder of the mountain man: Should he agree with Drew and notify the police, or should he agree with Lewis and bury the body? Cooper would not ask such questions because he would not pose such a quandary. Although a man of the wilderness, Natty recognizes the rules of the town. He always knows how to act. But Dickey characterizes Ed as a modern Chingachgook caught in a postmodern predicament. Stripped of the opportunity to call on the familiar props of easily discernible right and wrong that he relies on in the city, Ed does not know what to do. Significantly, then, the identification between beast and male is made explicit once he accepts Lewis's plan, agrees to bury the corpse, and thereby elevates the urge to survive over the moral considerations of murder.

As they hide the body, Dickey describes their actions in a sentence so simple that one can overlook it because of the tension of the scene: "Lewis went up the far bank like a creature" (133). Dickey then shifts the simile to Ed: "I got on my back and poured with the river, sliding over the stones like a creature I had always contained but never released. . . . Over the stones I slid over like a moccasin" (144). Ed attains his goal of sliding, but he now slides with the facility of a water mocassin instead of with the avoidance of friction dictated by a gentlemanly code of manners. He realizes that he is no longer an unprepared man from the city but an "out-of-shape animal" in the woods. He too lifts his forepaw, something that Natty would never do and that Ed's wife would not recognize. Now that he has discovered the line or border between beast and human, he must cultivate and release his animal nature before he can confront the comparable bestiality of his unseen antagonist, the second mountain man.

Aware of Lawrence's description of the American literary hero as "isolate," Dickey places Ed in "the most entire aloneness that [he] had ever been given" (161). With Lewis incapacitated, Drew dead, and Bobby useless, Ed begins to enjoy a duel in which the eventual survivor will have to exhibit superior animal-like characteristics instead of rationality. Dickey's added twist is that Ed is fully conscious of what he must do. Whereas earlier, while burying the corpse, he senses that his sliding into a creature-like state is gradual, now he deliberately cultivates his bestiality as he clings to the mountainside like a "burrowing animal," "like a creature born on the cliff and coming home" (177). His description of his plan of pursuit once he gains the top confirms his acceptance of what has happened to him: "When I finish that, I'll make a circle inland, very quiet, and look for him like I'm some kind of an animal. What kind? It doesn't matter, as long as I'm quiet and deadly. I could be a snake" (174). Here at long last is Cooper's Sarpent in postmodern America, Chingachgook writ large in the apotheosis of the novel of manliness, the Sarpent free of women except for a dream, and even free of Natty, but a Sarpent of diminished myth.

Dickey knows this, of course. He knows also that his contemporary Chingachgook is turning not evil, as the Edenic myth would identify the snake, but indifferent to killing, as Lawrence suggested he might: "An enormous physical indifference, as vast as the whole abyss of light at my feet, came to me: an indifference not only to the other man's body scrambling and kicking on the ground with an arrow through it, but also to mine" (180). Once Ed makes up his mind to uncage the beast, he develops the extrasensitivity that enhances his sight and smell and that allows him to detect where the mountain man is hiding. Dropping on all fours "like a dog," he tracks his wounded enemy by smelling the blood on the ground.

What saves *Deliverance* from being a John Wayne Western, a *Last of the Mohicans* without Cooper's vision, is the ambiguity that Dickey develops throughout. Like Cooper, Dickey is conscious of the always implied contrast between the moral considerations that regulate city life and the code of masculinity that determines wilderness death. This tension illustrates their approaches to culture, although Cooper envisions the founding while Dickey glimpses the decline. But where Cooper's bonded males identify their enemies with the certainty of righteousness, Dickey's are never so sure. In search of an Eden, however reduced, when they leave femininity and the town for masculinity and the forest, they find instead a post-Edenic ambiguity that perverts the pure nature of maleness which they have read about in classic American novels all their lives. Not only do men sexually violate men, but Ed confronts a question that he will have to ask forever: Has he killed the right man?

From the perspective of his bestial instincts, the correct identity does not matter. But from the point of view of his humanity, the question of identity is crucial. Equally important, and equally ambiguous, is whether Drew is killed by a bullet from the mountain man's rifle. If he is not, then Ed has no reason to kill anyone. These ambiguities rest at the heart of Dickey's re-reading of *The Last of the*

Mohicans. In a court of law, the very authority that Natty debates with Ishmael Bush in *The Prairie,* such unanswered queries would be of utmost importance. For without the distinctions between self-defense and murder, and between accidental death and premeditated killing—distinctions that Natty makes with relative ease—the moral priorities directing the civilized state that Ed is used to and that even Natty acknowledges would break down. But in a territory bordered on the one hand by rugged wilderness and on the other by a wild river, and where males maraud against males, fundamental distinctions are neutralized, and the niceties of various kinds of killing become meaningless: death is death. Unlike Cooper with Leatherstocking and Chingachgook, Dickey places Ed in a dilemma where prolonged discussion of the morality of his acts could result in his own death. Ed thinks that he must kill to avoid being killed. He could very well be wrong, but he believes the circumstances demand action rather than analysis. In Dickey's world, but not Cooper's, moral distinctions serve those who remain in or return to the settlement. Only bestial instincts can benefit the isolated, stoic, hard male when traditional morality is impotent.

Because Natty Bumppo's western horizon is unavailable to him, Ed must recross the border to reenter the city with its standard behavior, or remain in what he finally describes as "the land of impossibility" (277). Changed as Leatherstocking and Chingachgook never are, and confessing that he has experienced a strange joy in releasing the creature that he has always contained, he violates another directive of civilized mores when he refuses to tell the true story to his wife. The rest of his life, no matter how truly he lives it, will be based on a lie. The harmony of bestiality is within him.

The antifemale bias in the classic American novel that Cooper began and that Dickey extends has a curious closure in *Deliverance.* The female of dreams is dismissed, and the hero of tradition is depleted. The bonded males leave the wilderness to return home, the one still leery of sex, the other to his wife. Just as Lewis gives up the myth of immortality and accepts the reality of death, so Ed abandons the woman with the golden eye and embraces the solidity of marriage. He would like to watch the model "hold her breast once more, in a small space full of men" (277), but he knows now that perfect sex is a male fantasy belonging in the land of impossibility. Cooper's Cora must die because she taints the forest, and the model must be banished because she threatens the home. Dickey magnifies the double bind that the traditional male American novelist and his bonded men impose on women: If the female embodies passion and strength, she may perish in the wilderness or be abstracted to the neverland of myth; if she exhibits inhibition and dependence, she may live in the settlement or be excluded by the writer who tells the tale. Why this should be so, and why the American novel is changing, are the subjects of speculation in the following chapters.

Notes

1. Carolyn Heilbrun, "The Masculine Wilderness of the American Novel," *Saturday Review* 29 Jan. 1972: 41–44.
2. Carolyn Heilbrun, "Millet's Sexual Politics: A Year Later," *Aphra* 2 (Summer 1971): 40.
3. Russell J. Reising, *The Unusable Past: Theory and the Study of American Literature* (New York: Methuen, 1986).
4. D. H. Lawrence, *Studies in Classic American Literature* (1923; Garden City, NY: Doubleday, 1951).
5. R. W. B. Lewis, *The American Adam: Innocence, Tragedy, and Tradition in the Nineteenth Century* (Chicago: University of Chicago Press, 1955; Phoenix ed. 1958).
6. James Fenimore Cooper, *The Prairie*, ed. James P. Elliott (Albany: State University of New York Press, 1985) 14–15.
7. Leslie Fiedler, *Love and Death in the American Novel* (1960; New York: Meridian, 1964).
8. Joel Porte, *The Romance in America; Studies in Cooper, Poe, Hawthorne, Melville, and James* (Middletown, CT: Wesleyan University Press, 1969).
9. James Dickey, *Deliverance* (Boston: Houghton Mifflin, 1970).

Chapter Two

The Sources of Male Bonding:
Controversy and Debate

The standard, influential theories of American fiction have become controversial because of changing attitudes toward gender. In the American novel of the 1980s—at least as written by many white males—integrity of spirit can no longer depend on avoidance of flesh. The notion of woman as defiler but man as pure does not hold. Thus while the male in contemporary fiction may be an American Adam in R. W. B. Lewis's sense of the term, he nevertheless invites Eve to join him when he crosses the border from society to wilderness. Unlike the canonical American literary hero, the male in more recent novels pursues unlimited space but acknowledges restricting time. In other words, he accepts the lure of the wilderness but takes society in the guise of women with him. The old cultural mandate to "outwit" women is passé. To describe in another way the significant change in American fiction that I am arguing, contemporary novelists concede a perpetually falling America and thus decline to endorse the myth of a new Eden. To establish virtue is no longer to abandon women. Both genders are tarnished in the post-Edenic America of the 1980s. This is why female sexuality is celebrated in recent fiction in a manner that would dismay classic American writers. The loss of cultural aspiration may mean the end of the traditional literary hero, but it signals the beginning of a fresh evaluation of gender.

As I suggested in the last chapter, the antifemale bias in James Dickey's *Deliverance* results not from a thoughtless dismissal of women but from an inheritance of novelistic tradition. That a novel of the 1970s should feel the impact of the 1820s is not surprising when one considers the tenacious hold that classic American fiction has had on the national literary imagination. Despite the complaints by poststructuralists committed to re-reading the American novel, the tradition has not been entirely pernicious. A vital fiction and a stimulating critical theory have been two of its more fortunate expressions. Even more significant, perhaps, is that the development of the fiction has been tied to the definition of culture. American novels deemed worthy of inclusion in the canon have invariably illustrated and shaped whatever white males have considered American in the national experience.

Such a reading of culture, however, is bound to be subjective and thus restrictive. The unfortunate implication is that novels which do not illustrate the classic tradition are undeserving of canonization and are even, somehow, not entirely American. One of my points about *Deliverance* is that although it pushes the quintessential American novel to the extreme where men without women turn on each other for no apparent reason, it is, for all its contemporaneity, a nineteenth-century tale. *Deliverance* is both the finest and most disturbing re-creation of *The Last of the Mohicans* in American literature. But while these two novels are indisputably American according to the definitions offered by the theorists discussed in the previous chapter; and while, though published 150 years apart, both books speak to similar concerns about the development of the United States, the understanding of gender relationships expressed by Cooper and Dickey goes deeper than a mere illustration of the ingrained position that women keep the domestic in the kitchen and men seek the heroic in the forest. A discussion of relevant studies in anthropology, psychology, literary history, and feminist theory will suggest the complexity of the issue. Once again *The Last of the Mohicans* will serve as the prototypical novel.

I

Several years ago Nina Baym summarized the problems caused by the very critics whose analyses of the development of the American novel have had such a far-reaching effect on fiction, imagination, and culture. One of the calmer and more thoughtful commentators on the dispute, Baym distilled her perspective in an essay deliberately titled to make the point: "Melodramas of Beset Manhood: How Theories of American Fiction Exclude Women Authors."[1] She emphasizes the critics instead of the novelists, and she does not mince words in expressing her charge: "If one accepts current theories of American literature, one accepts as a consequence—perhaps not deliberately but nevertheless inevitably—a literature that is essentially male" (65). One could rebut, of course, that Baym shops to find a theory to fit her thesis, but more is at stake. With her protest clearly stated, she names standard works of American literary criticism—the very studies that originally shaped several generations' understanding of the tradition of the novel in the United States—and argues that such commentators as R. W. B. Lewis, Richard Chase, and Joel Porte have in mind not a representative sense of Americanness but "some qualitative essence."

The *essence* is qualitative because prevailing theories of American literature are committed to defining its uniqueness, its difference from European models, especially British. Surely D. H. Lawrence had such a goal in mind when, as an Englishman, he set out to dissect the literature of another country where he happened to be living at the time. But the result of these theoretical speculations is that novels which do not help to define the peculiar Americanness of the culture cannot meet certain specifications of excellence and thus are relegated to the dimmer corners of the canon. Novelists who probe the tensions of American experience turn out to be primarily white, middle class, and male.

Yet a greater issue, one finds, is not that women are excluded from the canon by novelists who depend on the special nature of Americanness for their subject matter but that women are largely omitted from the novels themselves. One thinks immediately of Cooper's long legacy: the Poe of *The Narrative of Arthur Gordon Pym* (1838), Melville, Twain, the Dos Passos of *Three Soldiers* (1921), the Cummings of *The Enormous Room* (1922), the Hemingway of the Nick Adams stories, the Faulkner of *Go Down, Moses* (1942), the Steinbeck of *Of Mice and Men* (1937), the Warren of *All the King's Men* (1946), the Mailer of *The Naked and the Dead* (1948), Jack Kerouac, Dickey. The list goes on. If novels about women are judged incapable of exploring the cultural tensions of the American essence, then the unavoidable result is that both the notion of America and the fiction that investigates it are oriented toward male bonding.

The paradigm is clear: women represent society; social forms are inimical to the glorification of the individual in the culture of the United States; thus the American literary hero must search for his integrity beyond the border, way off in the wilderness that Carolyn Heilbrun terms "masculine." How may one inscribe one's own destiny if one has a wife in the bedroom and children in the yard? To write *that* kind of novel would be to focus not on individual but on social concerns and thereby mimic the realistic novel of Great Britain and the continent. To write *that* kind of novel would be to substitute Susan Warner's *The Wide, Wide World* (1850) for *Moby-Dick*. To write *that* kind of novel would not be "American."[2] Canonical American fiction celebrates the individual opposed to rather than in society. The question is why.

To find an answer, I turn to sociology and anthropology. Nineteenth-century ideas of American manhood as illustrated by Cooper, Melville, and Twain were very much a part of the manner by which the fledgling nation sought to define its uniqueness. Gender ideals were largely determined by the burgeoning middle class; and as E. Anthony Rotundo has shown in his analysis of the diaries and correspondence of one hundred Northern middle-class males, the family unit, including both men and women, first shaped and then sustained the sense of manliness in the nineteenth century.[3] Drawing on Charles Rosenberg's essay "Sexuality, Class and Role in 19th-Century America," Rotundo identifies three models of manhood for American boys from 1800 to 1900: the Masculine Achiever, the Christian Gentleman, and the Masculine Primitive.[4] Despite the near-comical clichés conjured by Rotundo's designations, the three types were at one time valid ideals. The first two described standards of behavior for most of the century, while the third became important primarily after the Civil War.

The concept of the Masculine Achiever was linked to the development of capitalism and an expanding business class. Concerned with more than mere action, this ideal stressed self-advancement. Taking Rotundo's point, one notes that the glorification of self-advancement illustrated the celebration of individuality as defined by the myth of culture and the canonical novels that expressed the myth. To succeed by hard work and dogged persistence, the individual—male, of course—had finally to sever his ties with the domesticity of the parlor and the inhibitions of the community. Although Rotundo has in mind incipient business tycoons, one sees Natty Bumppo leaving home to stride beyond banks and counting houses to pursue the immortality of myth in the mortal world of the mundane. His uncompromising independence separates him from Duncan Heyward who, in committing to Alice Munro, exchanges the lessons taught in the forest for the security learned in the home. "Accomplishment, autonomy, and aggression," characteristics for success in the new American marketplace, were eerily close to the qualities that D. H. Lawrence deemed integral to the spirit of the American literary hero. Male expression of feeling was tantamount to capitulating to female sentimentality. Tenderness was relegated to church, kitchen, and community; that is, to women. The bonded males, Natty and Chingachgook, may not cry when their son Uncas dies.

Although the United States was rugged and untamed when the goal of Masculine Achiever was judged exemplary for American males, the influence of the family forced a revision of the ideal. Rotundo shows that the model of Christian Gentleman was developed as an antidote for the ruthlessness of the male achiever. If communal values lose their mandate entirely, moral values lose their force. The result is individuality run wild, the idea of America without the ideal. Cooper's Ishmael Bush personifies the notion of the Masculine Achiever taken to the extreme, and for his sins he loses a son and is pulled back to the settlement by the power of matriarchy. Ironically, in extending the goal of male aggressiveness to the limit, Bush forfeits his masculinity.

Compassion and sacrifice rather than aggression and gain were the characteristics of the Christian Gentleman. The irony is, however, that the antidote became the blender, and the models of Achiever and Gentleman were united in order to accommodate the dual pursuits of worldly success and moral behavior. Similarly, one suggests, the literary heroes on whom theories of American fiction are based assimilate both standards of manly excellence. For all his prowess with a rifle and his sagacity in the woods, Natty never tires of appealing to the Great Spirit or of treating women with the courtesy of a priest. He is a gentleman of the forest, quick to kill and eager to pray. Unlike Ishmael Bush, he combines the two ideals and avoids compromising his maleness. Little wonder that the unity of manliness and morality stands behind Cooper's Leatherstocking, Melville's Ishmael, and Twain's Huck Finn.

Rotundo shows that the Masculine Primitive, the third model, had little in common with the values and development of the two other prototypes of American masculinity. The nineteenth century stressed that civilized men, much more than women, resembled savages, especially in such stressful predicaments as combat, and that natural instinct and physical strength were to be encouraged as means of taking advantage of male primitiveness. Rotundo quotes, for example, a Union officer in the Civil War who thought of Cooper's Indians when scouting a bullet-raked knoll that he had to cross. There is no question that Cooper taught generations of readers the proper gender roles of the day. The Union officer might also have remembered Natty or Ishmael, for the combination of masculinity and morality found in the American Primitive was immortalized for the emerging nation not in some long-forgotten business tycoon but in the heroes who shaped the American myth through literature.

Although American businessmen in the mid nineteenth century may have used the wilderness as a metaphor for the marketplace while they selected from among the three definitions of manhood to guide their treks into the wild, American novelists of the period idealized the wilderness as the domain of potentially limitless territory. They understood, however indirectly, that survival in the forest depended on a unity of the three ideals. The Leatherstocking tales helped define the American imagination, for Cooper's portrait of the white hunter endowed with primitive strength, rational skills, and religious surety personified what Rotundo describes as "the popularity of the metaphor in which a man's life was a competitive jungle struggle and the pride in the physical combativeness of young men" (42). Unlike the models of Achiever and Gentleman that were glorified in letters and diaries following the American Revolution, the Masculine Primitive became an accepted standard of behavior in the middle third of the nineteenth century *after* Cooper had Americanized the archetype.

The gender issue was not always exclusive, of course, but Rotundo's study of family letters of the era shows that mothers and fathers wrote to the same son from opposed perspectives on manliness. Urging the ideal of the Christian Gentleman, for example, mothers counseled moral character and a good heart. Praising the ideal of the Masculine Achiever, fathers advised perseverance and strength. The sons who received these missives responded in kind. Thanking the father for advice on how to avoid failure in the wilderness of the businessplace that loomed beyond the hearth, the young man would simultaneously bless the mother for "godly prayers" and "pious exhortations" as he stretched the apron strings that held him (44). One understands why American novels of the nineteenth century were written along generally divided gender lines. Melville both celebrates and criticizes Ahab for wrecking vengeance on the dumb brute that ruins his body and sears his soul, but Mrs. Stowe disavows violence and salutes Tom for meeting brutality with prayer. Both literary heroes achieve myth, and both propose standards of manly behavior, but given the then-current instruction in masculinity and morality, one sees how the response to gender helped to shape American culture through fiction. That the separate teaching roles of mother and father were not mutually exclusive is important to the study of social history, but it is not the point here. What matters for the moment is that, generally, fathers wrote letters to sons that recommended male ideals similar to those mythologized by canonical American novelists. Perseverance hardened by moral fiber and physical strength was considered mandatory for the child who would be successful upon negotiating the border beyond the home. One hardly need reiterate that in nineteenth-century America very few daughters left home except to cross the yard to another parlor.

The pervasive influence of male bonding illustrated by American fiction and by the critical theory that explains it has anthropological roots. In *The Imperial Animal*, Lionel Tiger and Robin Fox include two sections that are significant to speculations about the American novel: "Bond Issue One: Women and Children First" and "Bond Issue Two: Man to Man."[5] Darwinians and behaviorists, Tiger and Fox investigate regularities of human action, what they term "the behavioral biogrammer." Thus when they make the controversial points that "war and fighting and the hunt have always been the business of human males, just as the protection of the troop is the business of male primates," and that "women are always a potential source of disruption to the unity, loyalty, and trust necessary to comrades in arms," they indicate that gender concerns are ephemeral (57). The authors of many canonical American novels would accept this position, even if indirectly, and thus I want simultaneously to discuss Tiger and Fox's theories of man-the-hunter and to suggest that representative male novelists of the 1980s disagree. The issue for readers of American literature is not the potential antipathy between the sexes but the difficulty of sustaining more than one major bond. If male bonding is necessary for the protection and survival of the group, as writers from Cooper to Dickey show it to be, then male-female relationships will always assume secondary importance. Uncas dies, not just because he desires a woman of another race but also because his desire for *any* woman threatens his obligatory bonding with Natty and Chingachgook. Tiger and Fox's basic point is that "all social acts are patterned." The primary regulations of any species are called *bonds*, and social bonding tempers randomness in social life. More important, bonding reduces the threat of aggression among members of the group: "The more highly developed the species, the more likely there is to be a high degree of individualism and aggressiveness, and hence of mistrust, and consequently of bonding" (58, 60). In the American novel, male bonding is normally the result of anxiety.

The mother-child bond is substantially different, as Harriet Beecher Stowe and Susan Warner—and Hawthorne—understand. To say that it is the most basic tie of all human bonding may be debatable, but Tiger and Fox stress nature's ruthlessness in insisting on the bond. Excessive separation of mother and child is devastating, especially for the child, who, as a result, may be incapable of forming permanent bonds when it matures. Tiger and Fox argue that social responses, often based on the mother-child bond, involve genetic programming. Rather than merely instinctive, behavioral patterns are social, depend on other members of the group, and reveal the evolutionary history of a species. Thus the family is not a natural unit of society but a social grouping. This opinion runs counter to that of other social scientists, but Tiger and Fox insist that the family is an artificial unit designed to enclose the basic bonding between mother and child. The absence or presence of males in the family group is of secondary importance: "The great variety and depth of customs surrounding kinship and marriage are not expressions of an innate and ready tendency to form families: *they are devices to protect the mother-child unit from the potential fragility of the mating bond*" (71).

Although I have simplified Tiger and Fox's sophisticated discussion, their analysis of the mother-child relationship serves as a frame for a study of male bonding. Like many anthropologists and sociobiologists, they trace the social acceptance of the division of labor between the sexes to the advent of organized hunting. Males killed game; females gathered grain. One understands how the Masculine Achiever and the Masculine Primitive could overwhelm the ideal of the Christian Gentleman in traditional American fiction. Disputing other theories which posit that sexual competition among males had to be eliminated in order for cooperation, hunting, and defense of the group to succeed, Tiger and Fox suggest that sexual rivalry was never negated but only "reworked" once food was determined the primary necessity. What Tiger and Fox call "a startling development" occurred when males needed to control the females of their own group in order to exchange them for the females of another group and thereby achieve both sexual satisfaction and political (territorial) advantage. The radical result—and a result with significant though indirect consequences for the American novel—was bonding between men who had been previously unrelated, especially the bonding of father-in-law and son-in-law, and of brothers-in-law. Different groups of males became dependent on one another for females and offspring; that is, for the survival of the social unit. Borrowing from Lévi-Strauss, Tiger and Fox are clear: "This principle of 'out marriage' is technically called 'exogamy,' and is the basis for all human kinship systems. . . . 'We will give our women to you if you give yours to us' " (89). Cooper's Magua has this principle in mind when his fight to marry Cora triggers his vow to destroy Uncas. Uncas feels an identical compulsion, but Cooper cannot tolerate such potential bonding given his understanding of male friendship beyond the clearing. Not sexual need but social control is the issue: "Marriage is one human institution allocating this control over women and offspring, and making it effective" (90).

What all this often means, of course, is that "no woman is as important to any man as men are to one another. . . . At all times and in all places men form groups from which they exclude women" (93–94). Such an attitude is not mere chauvinism, as the classic American novelists realized, for from the point of view of the social unit the male-male bond is as important as the mother-child bond. If Uncas takes Cora with him into the wilderness, or if Ed Gentry invites the model with the golden eye to the wild river, the mutual defense of the male group and by extension the welfare of society would break down. That Uncas is the last of the Mohicans and thus in need of offspring is of little consequence when one considers that Cooper has formed the new social unit of Natty and Chingachgook to protect both the ideal of America and the English settlers who are destined to replace the depleted Mohicans. Today's political pressure to the contrary, Tiger and Fox insist that male bonding is vital to society. In a statement that may anger some readers but that would hardly faze classic American writers, they observe of male bonding: "As a process, it reflects what we are, and how we evolved as primates uniquely skilled at gluing symbols onto relationships. This should make us as skeptical about the elimination of this bonding tendency as we would be of seriously curtailing heterosexual activity" (97).

Needless to say, Tiger and Fox question the currently fashionable notion that male conspiracy keeps females politically subservient. Convinced that many gender differences, both physiological and behavioral, are biologically based, they suggest that an example of male success in managing the nuances of male bonding is the preeminence of men in the political life of nearly every group. Much of this they trace to the early eons of the species when the development of hunting defined the social behavior of men and women. If one wants to change this situation with regard to gender—and it is clear today that change is necessary—one will have to alter behavioral patterns that have unfolded in most societies over millions of years. Equal participation of males and females in the politics of the group is a laudable goal, but Tiger and Fox stress that to achieve it one will have to "say 'no' to nature" and revise "a pattern bred into our behavior over the millennia. It may well be possible, but it will not be easy" (101). The issue, and it is an important one for studying recent American novelists, is that society must learn to act not against but within gender differences if the political process is to be altered. Rhetoric in the name of equality is beside the point.

To support their understanding of gender differences, Tiger and Fox observe a crucial distinction between female and male bonding.

The community helps the female achieve the social status of woman because it recognizes the physiological change signaled by menstruation. Males have a more difficult time. Since physical maturity is not enough for a male to be judged a man, the male must demonstrate by performance that he is worthy of bonding with males already initiated. This is a primary reason, I suggest, that initiation stories invariably describe the plight of young men rather than of young women, and why the wilderness, the metaphorical arena of trial and success or failure, is invaded most often by men. Cooper accepts these notions of bonding, as he shows with Cora and Alice Munro. Postmenstrual and sexually potent, Cora is accepted as a woman by both genders and has no need to prove her maturity. Alice is another matter. Characterizing her as dependent to the point of helplessness, Cooper makes her metaphorically premenstrual and, except for her half-sibling, bonded to no one. Both females are out of place in the wilderness, the proving ground of male performance, but Alice would also be a weakling in the town. Cooper shows that Alice must mature before her bond with women is automatically sealed. Duncan Heyward spells out the difference between the sisters: "To you, Cora, I will urge no words of idle encouragement; your own fortitude and undisturbed reason, will teach you all that may become your sex; but cannot we dry the tears of that trembling weeper on your bosom?"[6]

Validation of the gender role is an arduous process for males, however, as literature has shown and social science confirmed. Alice merely needs to stop weeping, but Heyward must prove his worthiness to act on Cooper's vision of the new society by learning from, keeping up with, and all but equaling Natty Bumppo and Chingachgook. Thus while the recent encouraging of women to venture beyond the home is socially equitable and politically correct, it means a radical change in well-established bonding practices. More important, write Tiger and Fox, it signals that "females have joined a system of long-term oppression, one of the functions of which is to induce young males to spend a long time learning particular practices vaguely related to adult statuses, and committing themselves to the structures of the adult males from whom all blessings flow" (112). To rephrase in terms of the novelists discussed later, do women truly want to enter the masculine wilderness, and what happens to male bonding when women leave the clearing? Ironically, what is perceived as male freedom is really male oppression of males. The rigors of male bonding are so extreme that men finally persecute men. Canonical American novelists have generally illustrated this truth. For all his Apollo-like prowess, for example, Uncas must prove himself to Natty and Chingachgook when Cora and Alice cross the border, just as un-prepared Ed Gentry must verify his masculinity to Lewis Medlock. The unexpected result is that Uncas fails the test when he desires Cora, and thus dies; while Ed passes the trial when he confirms his bestiality, and thus lives. That Uncas is the better man is not the question. The point is that the last Mohican finally does not meet the requirements of male bonding.

Neither do many other American literary heroes. Although they may survive, as Melville wrote, to trace the round again, they fail the rigors of the bond. Ishmael does not save Queequeg; Huck Finn does not keep Jim from prejudice; Jake Barnes does not help Pedro Romero; Ike McCaslin does not live up to Sam Fathers; Nick Carra-way does not protect Gatsby; Sal Paradise does not locate Dean Mo-riarty's father; Herbert Stencil and Benny Profane do not find V.; Skipper and Sonny do not prevent Cassandra's suicide. The presence of women complicates the process of bonding even further. Studies of various societies reveal that one strong bonding relationship precludes another. American novelists illustrate this, however intuitively or em-pirically, especially Cooper, who has Leatherstocking explain how his loyalty to one bond prohibits his accepting another:

> I have heard . . . that there is a feeling in youth, which binds man to woman, closer than the father is tied to the son. It may be so. I have seldom been where women of my colour dwell; but such may be the gifts of natur in the settlements! You have risked life, and all that is dear to you, to bring off this gentle one, and I suppose that some such disposition is at the bottom of it all. As for me, I taught the lad the real character of a rifle; and well has he paid me for it! I have fou't at his side in many a bloody skrimmage; and so long as I could hear the crack of his piece in one ear, and that of the Sagamore in the other, I knew no enemy was on my back.[7]

Male-female bonding may be the business of life, but Natty (and Cooper) realizes that male-male bonding is a matter of life and death.

It is not merely that Cora and Alice bring the taint of sex and the threat of domesticity into the wilderness, but that they confuse the complex system of male relationships that center on the bonds of father-son (Chingachgook and Uncas), surrogate father and son (Natty and Uncas; Natty and Heyward), and surrogate brother and brother (Uncas and Heyward; Natty and Chingachgook; and even Uncas and Magua). Note how Natty stresses men but not women when he speaks of the promise of an afterlife: "I loved both you and your father, Uncas, though our skins are not altogether of a colour, and our gifts are somewhat different. Tell the Sagamore I never lost sight of him in my greatest trouble . . . and depend on it, boy, whether there be one heaven or two, there is a path in the other world, by which honest men may come together, again."[8] Cora must die within the masculine wilderness, and Alice removed from it, if intense male bonds are to endure. Natty even implies that women are to be excluded from heaven since they are responsible for the Fall. For Uncas to settle down with Cora at Glenn's Falls, and Duncan Heyward with Alice, would be to read *The Last of the Mohicans* as *The Little House on the Prairie*.

II

As Natty's comment implies, women are a complicating factor, but no male can survive in the forest alone. He must have allies, men he can depend on and who depend on him. Such bonding guarantees the safety of brotherhood, but it also promises the peril of obligation. Leatherstocking accepts this burden without quarrel, but Melville's Ishmael must learn it to his chagrin. In the famous chapter "The Monkey-Rope," Ishmael understands the complexities of bonding for the first time:

> Queequeg was my own inseparable twin brother; nor could I any way get rid of the dangerous liabilities which the hempen bond entailed. So strongly and metaphysically did I conceive of my situation then, that while earnestly watching his motions, I seemed distinctively to perceive that my own individuality was now merged in a joint stock company of two; that my free will had received a mortal wound; and that another's mistake or misfortune might plunge innocent me into unmerited disaster and death.[9]

Although Ishmael calls bonding "so gross an injustice," he soon realizes that his situation is universal.

Psychologists use the term *attachment* to describe the special bonding of Ishmael and Queequeg and of Natty and Chingachgook. As Mary D. Salter Ainsworth explains, "Like other basic behavioral systems, attachment behavior is believed to have evolved through a process of natural selection because it yielded a survival advantage."[10] She goes on to demonstrate that affectional bonds differ from relationships primarily because the former are much more likely to last, and she defines the affectional bond as "a relatively long-enduring tie in which the partner is important as a unique individual and is interchangeable with none other. . . . Inexplicable separation tends to cause distress, and permanent loss would cause grief" (711).

In literary criticism the word currently used to account for male attachments is *homosocial*. Writing from a feminist perspective, Eve Kosofsky Sedgwick analyzes the term to discuss primarily English literature and British culture from the mid-eighteenth to the mid-nineteenth centuries.[11] Yet her discussion is relevant to my analysis because she distinguishes between homosocial and homosexual bonding. She also argues that in British society the development of male friendship, with its extremes of mentorship and rivalry, was based on a pattern of shifting relations to social class; and that the entire system of gender must be recognized if one is to understand the complexity of male bonding.

Because the society depicted in the American novel is generally middle class, several of Sedgwick's observations need not be discussed, but her thorough definition of *homosocial* is useful:

> "Homosocial" is a word occasionally used in history and the social sciences, where it describes social bonds between persons of the same sex; it is a neologism, obviously formed by analogy with "homosexual," and just as obviously meant to be distinguished from "homosexual." In fact, it is applied to such activities as "male bonding," which may, as in our society, be characterized by intense homophobia, fear and hatred of homosexuality (1).

Homosexuality is not a primary issue in American fiction (it is more so in American poetry), and thus homophobia and fear are usually only undercurrents in the novels analyzed here.

Nevertheless, Sedgwick's suggestion of a continuum between homosocial and homosexual is of interest: "a continuum whose visibility, for men, in our society, is radically disrupted" (1–2). Selecting from Lacan the term *desire* rather than *love* to stress the erotic nature of the homosocial bond, she is concerned with how far the cultural force of homosocial desire is "properly sexual." Leslie Fiedler broaches this topic in *Love and Death in the American Novel*, but he is not interested in the full spectrum of gender issues. Sedgwick is, and to support her thesis she points out—correctly, it seems to me—that the opposition between homosocial and homosexual is less dichotomous for women than for men. Despite the discontinuities of race and class, women who promote the interest of other women, in whatever form, pursue "congruent and closely related activities" (3). One need not contrast homosocial and homosexual when discussing female bonding, for both contribute to a continuum of women's concerns.

Such is not the case with men. As discussed earlier, male bonding is much more difficult to achieve than female attachment. One cause of the difficulty is that society is traditionally patriarchal, and, as Sedgwick observes, most forms of patriarchy are homophobic. Thus homophobia is as much a "necessary consequence" of social forms as heterosexual marriage: "Our own society is brutally homophobic; and the homophobia directed against both males and females is not arbitrary or gratuitous, but tightly knit into the texture of family, gender, age, class, and race relations. Our society could not cease to be homophobic and have its economic and political structures remain unchanged" (3–4). One need not agree with Sedgwick's rhetoric to understand that the social issue, as always, is power. Heterosexuality threatens Natty's retreating Eden, and homosexuality menaces Ed Gentry's shrunken wilderness. In both cases of male bonding the dilemma concerns the ultimate control of people and nature.

Different political circumstances will always define whether homosexual affinities oppose or support homosocial bonding. The connection between sexual alienation and political power is not stable but volatile, and Sedgwick correctly urges rejecting simplistic definitions of the relationships between the two. For this reason she avoids reading sexual bonding in British literature from either a Marxist feminist (historical) or radical feminist (structuralist) point of view, preferring instead to combine the two so that ideology can be used as a means of analyzing sexuality: "What *counts* as the sexual is . . . variable and itself political." Her point is that the European literary heritage "as it exists" is a male-homosocial canon, and "most so when it is most heterosexual" (15, 17). Citing René Girard's *Deceit, Desire, and the Novel,* Sedgwick discusses how, in erotic triangles, "the bond that links the two rivals is as intense and potent as the bond that links either of the rivals to the beloved" (21). One sees this level of homosocial rivalry in *The Last of the Mohicans* in a male bonding that is rarely discussed, that of Uncas and Magua. The two young chiefs of alien tribes are drawn to each other in enmity not because their nations are at war but because they desire the same woman. That both die as a result is Cooper's logical conclusion to the bond. Neither male may have the female in Cooper's mythic and cultural scheme.

The beloved is often the object of desire primarily because she has already been chosen by the rival. Girard stresses what Sedgwick calls "the male-centered novelistic tradition" of European high culture. The bonds that interest him are between two males who compete for a female. One notes immediately the symmetry of his paradigm, a symmetry that does not account for what Sedgwick defines as the asymmetry of "the radically disrupted continuum, in our society, between sexual and nonsexual male bonds, as against the relatively smooth and palpable continuum of female homosocial desire" (23). Such asymmetry would challenge the pat erotic triangle of two men bonding in pursuit of the same woman.

Sedgwick's analysis is an invaluable, indirect contribution to the continuing discussion about the definition of the American novel, and like all good criticism it prompts questions that one should like to ask even if one does not answer them completely. May homosocial literature, for example, challenge gender stereotypes? What happens when the bonds among a novelist's characters are not erotic? More important, is it possible that in contemporary American fiction the symmetry that Sedgwick detects in Girard's paradigm holds fast, and that what feminists complain of as the patriarchal heterosexuality of these novels depends on female characters who facilitate the bonding of the male protagonists?

Unlike the British novel, and with such obvious exceptions as James and Wharton, marriage is not generally an issue in canonical American literature. What matters is that the threat of female presence cements male bonding. But flight from the woman is no longer the agenda in contemporary fiction as it was in the nineteenth-century American novel. When the men in more recent fiction light out for the territory to escape the defilement by sex and the constraint of the home, they find that women are already there, waiting for them in the proverbial dark woods on the other side of civilization. The male homosocial bond—as opposed to homosexual—is not negated but strengthened, as it normally is in American fiction, but with the radical difference that the female is now inextricably part of the bonding. It is as if Cooper allowed Cora to walk westward with Natty and Chingachgook, or Dickey invited the model with the golden eye into the north Georgia hills with Ed Gentry and Lewis Medlock.

Ironically, masculinity is enhanced rather than threatened. What the contemporary novels do not investigate, however, is whether the privileging of male bonding via the proximity of the female is damaging to women. Power defined by gender may still be a primary issue, and the wilderness of the American novel may continue to be a predominantly masculine domain, but women have very clearly entered the forest. Moreover, while some of these women have no inherent value except as currency in the exchange between men (*Billy Bathgate*), others are valuable in their own right and are celebrated for their own worth (*Sometimes I Live in the Country* and *A Prayer for Owen Meany*). This differentiation may explain why male bonding in *Billy Bathgate* involves mastery and subordination, while bonding in *Sometimes I Live in the Country* and *A Prayer for Owen Meany* resembles brotherhood. Brotherhood would seem to be the condition of male bonding when women are absent (*Moby-Dick*) or a threat (*The Last of the Mohicans*), or when women are more or less accepted as both necessary and equal (*Sometimes I Live in the Country*). But when the woman is little more than a commodity of exchange, as in *Billy Bathgate* where Billy's cuckolding of Dutch Schultz carries overtones of homosocial vengeance, male bonding veers toward the violence of master and subject. All three of these contemporary novels are violent, but whereas the violence of Busch's tale is racial, and that of Irving's fated, the violence of Doctorow's fiction is gender related. In *Billy Bathgate* males first brutalize females and then turn on each other. One wonders whether homophobia rather than the homosocial is the hidden agenda.

As Sedgwick suggests in her concluding chapter, "Toward the Twentieth Century: English Readers of Whitman," homophobic undermining of homosocial relationships has intensified in the twentieth century. Despite the intertextual affinities, the startling differences between *The Last of the Mohicans* and *Deliverance* illustrate the intensity and support the assertion that even a work like *In Memoriam* "would have had to be written very differently indeed by 1910" (201). Sedgwick's judgment of Tennyson and his age may be true, but what interests me is how representative American novels of the 1980s—all written by white, middle-class males—reassert the traditional ideal of male bonding as worked out in classic American fiction, but with the radical disruption that a woman makes a trio out of a duo.

III

I conclude this chapter with an observation on androgyny as a complement to the concept of the homosocial when discussing the American novel, and with a final comment on *The Last of the Mohicans*. Especially pertinent here is Carolyn Heilbrun's "Further Notes Toward a Recognition of Androgyny."[12] The essay is a follow-up to her study *Toward a Recognition of Androgyny* (1973), a necessary clarification because on publishing her book she learned that misunderstanding was bound to greet anyone who questioned the traditional views of "masculine" and "feminine." Lamenting that society is sexually polarized, she recommends androgyny as a way to heal the breach, and she defines the term as a "condition under which the characteristics of the sexes and the human impulses expressed by men and women are not rigidly assigned" (143). Thus androgyny facilitates not polarization but reconciliation to the extent that women may cultivate aggressiveness, men tenderness. In other words, custom or propriety would not determine gender behavior.

Reading such a recommendation, Tiger and Fox, as well as other biodeterminists, might respond that contemporary theoretical positions cannot alter ancient behavioral conditioning. Heilbrun's suggestion was not heeded. Rather, it was distorted to equate androgyny with homosexuality and bisexuality. Ignoring Coleridge's observation—which Heilbrun cites—that "a great mind must be androgynous," those who warped her definition refused to consider her position as anything other than "a physical or social anomaly." But anomaly is not the issue. Heilbrun refers for support to Jeanne Humphrey Block's analysis of the development of sex roles in America, which shows that the United States generally emphasizes "early and clear sex typing" while deemphasizing control of male aggressiveness.

Yet even scholars who sympathize with Heilbrun's concern dispute her position. Daniel A. Harris, for example, argues that "for feminist men as well as for feminist women, the myth of androgyny has no positive value."[13] He insists that androgyny maintains sexist polarizations to define identity, and he criticizes Heilbrun for failing to "recognize the tradition of negative attitudes towards men and women which the history of the myth . . . embodies" (173–74). Barbara Charlesworth Gelpi is even more direct when she warns that the ideal of androgyny was originally created by men and always assumes women's inferiority.[14]

Confronted with such feminist criticism, one recalls D. H. Lawrence's definition of the isolated male and heroic killer in American literature. More important, one remembers that Cooper must remove Cora from the masculine wilderness of the American novel, not merely because she dares to love Uncas and thus would confuse misogyny with miscegenation, but also because her valor and strength combine with her obvious sexuality to cast her as androgynous and thereby a threat to the homosocial bond of Natty and Chingachgook. Their mythic friendship is always remembered and justly admired, but one does not forget that Cora indirectly destroys other bonds because of her androgyny: Uncas-Cora, Magua–Cora, Uncas–Duncan Heyward, Uncas–Chingachgook, and Cora–Alice. The only other bond to survive is that of Alice and Duncan, but they must retreat from the forest if they hope to live. More significant, in my opinion, is that Cooper knew that Cora's androgyny also menaces the status of the purely feminine Alice. As Cooper's choice for the role of the matriarch of America, blonde, weak, tender Alice may not be left for long in proximity to her dark, strong, aggressive sister. To do so would be to confuse gender roles for the woman who, by supporting her future husband, is to bring male-defined standards of maternity and domesticity from the settled east coast to the heart of American savagery.

To read Cooper and the American novel as I have suggested in these chapters is to commit oneself to re-reading the canon. Natty and Chingachgook are indeed the mythic heroes of *The Last of the Mohicans* as well as the prototypes for male performance in American fiction. Yet one wonders whether Cora is the moral center, or at least the potential moral center, of the emerging nation, if only Cooper would celebrate her androgyny and offer it as a personification of the possibility for a true difference between the about-to-be-born United States and the already-old Europe. But Cooper reads in the early nineteenth century as many do in the late twentieth century: the primary energy in a novel and, one assumes, in a culture must generally be centered in the male. Duncan Heyward, Alice's future husband and the symbolic father of America, earns his authority as the new leader of the civilization advancing from the east not by adapting to Alice's tenderness but by assimilating Natty's aggressiveness. If he wants sex with Alice, he must marry her. If she desires marriage with Duncan, she must have sex. His strength and her weakness will then be complementary, but they will never be merged. Cora bursts the bounds of these gender roles and must die. All that Leatherstocking and Chingachgook can do is reaffirm their bond and escape farther west.

Notes

1. Nina Baym, "Melodramas of Beset Manhood: How Theories of American Fiction Exclude Women Authors," *The New Feminist Criticism: Essays on Women, Literature, and Theory*, ed. Elaine Showalter (New York: Pantheon, 1985) 63–80.
2. For an analysis of the importance of realistic social fiction in the United States of the nineteenth century, see Alfred Habegger, *Gender, Fantasy, and Realism in American Literature* (New York: Columbia University Press, 1982).
3. E. Anthony Rotundo, "Learning about Manhood: Gender Ideals and the Middle-Class Family in Nineteenth-Century America," *Manliness and Morality: Middle-Class Masculinity in Britain and America 1800–1940*, ed. J. A. Mangan and James Walvin (Manchester: Manchester University Press, 1987) 35–51.
4. Charles Rosenberg, "Sexuality, Class and Role in 19th-Century America," *The American Male*, ed. Elizabeth Pleck and Joseph H. Pleck (Englewood Cliffs, NJ: Prentice-Hall, 1980) 219–54.

5. Lionel Tiger and Robin Fox, *The Imperial Animal* (New York: Holt, Rinehart and Winston, 1971).

6. James Fenimore Cooper, *The Last of the Mohicans*, ed. James Franklin Beard, James A. Sappenfield, and E. N. Feltskog (Albany: State University of New York Press, 1983) 82.

7. *The Last of the Mohicans*, 265.

8. *The Last of the Mohicans*, 315.

9. Herman Melville, *Moby-Dick* (Evanston and Chicago: Northwestern University Press and The Newberry Library, 1988) 320.

10. Mary D. Salter Ainsworth, "Attachments Beyond Infancy," *American Psychologist* 44 (April 1989) 709–16.

11. Eve Kosofsky Sedgwick, *Between Men: English Literature and Male Homosocial Desire* (New York: Columbia University Press, 1985).

12. Carolyn Heilbrun, "Further Notes Toward a Recognition of Androgyny," *Women's Studies* 2 (1974): 143–49.

13. Daniel A. Harris, "Androgyny: The Sexist Myth in Disguise," *Women's Studies* 2 (1974): 171–84.

14. Barbara Charlesworth Gelpi, "The Politics of Androgyny," *Women's Studies* 2 (1974): 151–60.

Chapter Three

The Politics of Male Bonding:
Sociobiology and Feminist Anthropology

Canonical American novelists generally celebrate what Lionel Tiger calls in another context "men in groups."[1] Writing in 1969, and likely aware of the political power of the newest wave of feminism, Tiger suggests that "the exclusion of females from certain categories of all-male groups reflects not only a formalized hostility to females but a positive valence, or 'attraction,' between males" (xiv). In his remarks on the role of the male bond in aggression he defines aggression as "a process of more or less conscious coercion against the will of any individual or group of animals or men by any individual or group of people" (158). The key to his definition is the distinction between aggression and violence, for the latter is only one possible result of the former. Aggressive behavior may not be violent, but it is always coercive. Its goal is mastery, as American novelists have always known.

I

Linking aggressive behavior to the development of hunting as a crucial step in evolution, Tiger insists that "human aggression in its social organizational sense is a propensity of males" and is stimulated when males associate primarily with other males (160). In other words, aggression is generally a gender rather than a human characteristic. This issue is debatable, but to illustrate his position with a literary model Tiger refers to William Golding's *Lord of the Flies* (1954), a novel with no female characters that identifies aggression and male bonding as allied processes. Tiger is direct: "In both violent and aggressive action male bonding is the predominant instrument of organization. Females tend to be excluded from aggressive organizations. . . . They do not form groups which are expressly devoted to violent activity or to potentially violent action" (171–72).

The point is that the presence of male bonding alone may cause aggressive behavior between bonded men and outside agencies. Suggesting that the relationship between male groups and aggression is more powerful than the sexual bond, Tiger argues that "aggression and violence, then, are not individually motivated behaviour patterns. They are 'released' or 'directed' by social activity, and particularly effectively so by the social interactions of males" (172). If Tiger is correct, then he has indirectly commented on the sexually immaculate behavior in the homosocial friendships of the traditional American novel. Sexual relationships with women are not commitments to the "weaker" sex but violations of a stronger bond. Male bonding is thus both a cause and function of aggression. Unlike women, men require the validation of masculinity that is achieved by bonding, a validation normally repeated throughout a man's life. This is why such novels as *The Last of the Mohicans* and *Deliverance* are rife with episodes of violent action. The multiple scenes of aggression are not gratuitous and surely not the result of the generally episodic structure of these novels; rather they are illustrations of the continuing male need to ratify maleness. According to man-the-hunter theories, the evolutionary facts are that males bond and that bonded males are aggressive. As Tiger observes, and as traditional American novelists intuit, "To reduce opportunities for such aggression is to tamper with an ancient and central pattern of human behaviour" (190–91).

All this does not mean, however, that violent relationships between groups of males are inevitable. Society can apply pressure when it has to, as in the United States of the nineteenth century when the concept of the Christian gentleman was devised to temper the behavior of the masculine achiever. "It may be possible," Tiger admits, "to alter social conceptions of maleness so that gentility and equivocation rather than toughness and more or less arbitrary decisiveness are highly valued" (191). To effect such a variation would be to revise the reward system. Honor and prestige would have to be allocated to less truculent males who do not feel as strongly the evolutionary need to prove their leadership legitimate. Such a change, however, would not deny that males find satisfactions in male interactions that they cannot derive from male-female interactions. Men bond in a variety of situations. More important, writes Tiger:

> They consciously and emotionally *exclude* females from these bonds. The significant notion here is that these broad patterns are biologically based, and that those variously different expressions of male dominance and male bonding in different communities are what one would expect from a species highly adaptable to its physical and social environments, and where learning is a crucial adaptive process (112).

My point is that current American writers need not neutralize the bonding process, as some feminists and utopians have urged; they need only adapt it, as many recent male novelists have done.

The issues of masculinity and femininity in society and literature are far from settled, and thus one is not surprised that Tiger's conclusions have been questioned by contemporary sociologists and sociobiologists. Tim Carrigan, Bob Connell, and John Lee, for example, accuse Tiger of ignoring the influence of social structure. Pointing out how accepting a "simple continuity" between the biological and the social generates an influential ideology, they dismiss Tiger's observations as "pseudo-evolutionary speculation."[2] Such disagreements among anthropologists and sociologists are likely to continue for some time, though with, one hopes, a more restrained rhetoric. Carmen Schifellite shows such restraint. Schifellite criticizes biodeterminist arguments as "misleading and simplistic, not to mention dangerous," because they organize human beings into convenient subgroups.[3] Observing that biologically deterministic theories originate in the "structured inequality of the societies that produce them," he suggests that both the science and the ideology of these societies encourage hypotheses that stress the apparent differences between various groups and subgroups. The likely result is that variations in behavior and habits will be attributed to "some type of immutable 'human nature' " (46).

This is not the place to discuss the nuances of Schifellite's censure of patriarchy, but one should understand that evolutionary theory borrowed from conservative capitalist ideology in the second half of the nineteenth century to legitimize various kinds of inequality in such supposedly egalitarian societies as Great Britain and the United States. In recent years sociobiology has emerged as the discipline that argues for genetic programming of human behavior. Although he agrees that the conclusions of sociobiologists are not as "crudely formulated" as nineteenth-century theories, Schifellite does not shrink from arguing that the effects of contemporary sociobiology "are not altogether different from its nineteenth-century forerunners" (49). One can see the general results of sociobiological hypotheses: the biological subsumes the social, and social institutions are attributed to genetic adaptations. One can also see a specific result: aggressive, rational males and nurturing, emotional females are deemed biological norms. One is suddenly back in the milieu of Natty Bumppo and Alice Munro.

But as Schifellite shows, and as many American novelists of the 1980s understand, "facts" are often selected to fit theories once a biological or evolutionary paradigm is established. Social biases, usually unintended, are thus ignored, and stereotypes of gender constrain behavior to the extent that they perpetuate themselves. The challenge to these stereotypes by contemporary male novelists is as indirect as Schifellite's conclusion is blunt:

> It is unclear that the separation between biology and environment is in any way useful. It may be popular, and it may be politically expedient, but it seems to be only marginally enlightening. Even if measurable differences are found to exist and can be shown to be sex-related and biodetermined, these findings will not automatically justify the inequality between the sexes. They will merely indicate differences. (60)

These differences affect literature, as Peter Schwenger has shown. Interested in the relationship between gender and fiction, Schwenger discusses the effect of masculine biases on writing by men.[4] His concerns are twentieth-century literature and literary style, and he is well aware of the dangers of identifying societal norms as biological facts. Like Patricia Meyer Spacks, he investigates how literary style has an "important relation" to sexual style, and he argues that style can both "render an existing sex role" and change it (3). His general point, and it is an important one, is that "the goal of manhood is less directly attainable in the twentieth century than ever" (8). Reaction to the pressure by females requires readjusting the definition of the male. The result is that a traditional understanding of manhood can no longer be assumed. Sociobiologists may disapprove, yet societal indicators suggest that "manhood is asserted as always, but never so easily as before" (9).

Late-twentieth-century assertions of masculinity have replaced early-nineteenth-century assumptions of patriarchy. Dickey asserts; Cooper assumes. The novelists I am concerned with do neither to an extreme because they have assimilated the changing prerogatives of gender that have largely resulted from the women's movement of the 1970s and 1980s. As Carrigan, Connell, and Lee note in their discussion of the sociology of masculinity, "Masculinity does move, sex roles have a history, and we are at one of its turning points" (156).

II

One of the reasons for the turning point is the feminist response to evolutionary theories of bonding which is fairly recent but already vast. Interested readers might consult the bibliography to the special issue on feminism and science in *Women's Studies International Forum* edited by Sue V. Rosser and dedicated to the memory of Ruth Bleier.[5] A medical doctor, Bleier was one of the first scholars in the United States to combine feminism and science in her research. Her major work, *Science and Gender: A Critique of Biology and Its Theories on Women*, is of special interest particularly because the chapter "Man the Hunter" questions the hypotheses argued by such anthropologists as Tiger and Fox.[6] Bleier concedes the widespread acceptance of bio-determinist theories that point to male bonding caused by the need to hunt as the central force in the origin of human society. But her concession is only to the currency of the biosocial position and not to its accuracy. She suggests, on the contrary, that man-the-hunter theories are primarily legitimating ideologies that enhance the authority traditionally assigned to males. The result is that post-Darwinian concepts of gender relationships are accepted as a natural consequence of human growth and thus as millions of years old.

As Bleier points out, the problem is that during the 1960s and 1970s "evolutionary reconstructions passed beyond speculation and hypotheses to become stated as fact" (120). The development of sociobiology as a relatively new academic discipline helped to consolidate the influence of man-the-hunter evolutionists, as illustrated primarily by Edward O. Wilson's *Sociobiology: The New Synthesis*.[7] For example, Wilson insists that aggression in humans is adaptive—"aggressive responses vary according to the situation in a genetically programmed manner"—and he describes males in the territory and females in the home as a biologically determined division (254–55, 533).[8] Challenging what she calls "Single Event hypotheses of the causality of any evolutionary phenomenon," Bleier argues that studies of human evolution will always privilege accounts of the necessity for male dominance so long as researchers overlook the fragmentary nature of the fossil record, especially since fossils traditionally associated with males (stone, bone, horn) have survived while those generally identified with females (plant, wood, bark) have disappeared (121). Thus she accuses biodeterminist anthropologists of ignoring contradictory evidence and of failing to indicate "the unknowns," and she questions the legitimacy of any theory that denigrates women in the account of *human*—as opposed to *male*—evolution. As she explains in another essay, males will "seek more and more the protection of presumed biological imperatives" as their power loses the authority of law and custom. In her view no behavioral pattern such as hunting can be called characteristically human.[9]

Citing such feminist scholars as Adrienne Zihlman and Nancy Tanner, Bleier offers alternatives to the man-the-hunter theory.[10] A thorough analysis of the complexities of her discussion would be inappropriate here, but I mention the high points to illustrate that the anthropological assumptions which have framed both gender constructs and American literature for decades are now being queried directly by female scientists and indirectly by male novelists.[11] The most significant alternative to what Bleier terms the "gender-dichotomous biocultural evolution" is the evidence that both men and women originally gathered plants and caught small animals in a social atmosphere free of pressure to engage in aggressive or competitive behavior (131). Bleier borrows here from Sally Slocum, who extends the theory of man-the-hunter to its extreme: "It leads to the conclusion that the basic human adaptation was the desire of males to hunt and kill."[12] In short, human society derives from killing. D. H. Lawrence would agree insofar as the myth of American culture is concerned. Urging a different account of evolution, Slocum says that an "unbiased" reading of the evidence shows that male bonding and hunting were not the foundations for the anthropological leap from protohominids to *Homo sapiens*. From the feminist perspective a more logical, more scientific theory is the increased time of infant dependence on the female: the longer that offspring remained dependent, the greater the area of the mother's gathering. Thus the family group relied for food not on bonding males but on gathering females.

Ben Greer is a male writer of the 1980s who balances bonded aggressors with the dominant presence of the female gatherer as the provider of food, and thus he modifies the American novel in the manner I have noted. In doing so he implies a shift of values in the relationship of gender as it has developed historically in American literature. As Donna J. Haraway observes, "Facts are theory laden; theories are value laden; values are history laden."[13] Although many scholars agree that the history of science is patriarchal, Haraway cautions feminist anthropologists to avoid "corrosive skepticism" toward science in the name of a new truth: "But the critique of bad science that glides into a radical doctrine that all scientific statements are historical fictions made facts through the exercise of power produces trouble when feminists want to talk about producing *feminist* science which is more *true*, not just better at predicting and controlling the body of the world" (478). Greer and most of the other contemporary novelists I cite avoid from a literary perspective the "corrosive" extreme that Haraway warns against, but one wonders whether Slocum does. Insistent to the point of seeming to acquiesce to a different bias, but a bias nonetheless, Slocum interprets male bonding from the opposite extreme of Tiger and Fox. Thus the spectrum is reversed, and another bond is privileged: "Food sharing and the family developed from the mother-infant bond" (45).

Bleier's balanced revisionism seems more helpful. If her conclusions about hunting are correct, then the long-accepted notion of males needing to bond in a territory beyond the hearth in order to ensure the survival of the social unit may be more anthropological fancy than evolutionary fact. Such a revision would have the far-reaching effect of challenging the historical accuracy on which the literary myth of an entire culture was founded. That novelists of the last two centuries have accepted, however obliquely, the primacy of male hunting is indisputable, as books as various as *The Last of the Mohicans*, *Moby-Dick*, the Nick Adams stories, and *Deliverance* show. Many American writers of the 1980s, however, question the assumptions about gender that such a theory inevitably advances, and thus they reflect changing social attitudes. Bleier concludes: "There is nothing intrinsic to hunting that distinguishes it from other social and cooperative forms of relationships around subsistence activities in its significance either for survival (except in very cold climates) or as a motive force in human cultural evolution" (132).

The debate between biodeterminists and sociobiologists on the one hand and feminist challengers regarding the meaning of male bonding on the other hand has generated a much needed new viewpoint on gender relationships. Canonical American writers have generally accepted the arguments for significant biological differences between the sexes and thus have written about eliminating women from the supposed male domain of the wilderness (*The Last of the Mohicans*) or have ignored women altogether (*Moby-Dick*.) Even if recent novelists have not specifically read the current scholarship in feminist anthropology, they cannot help but be aware of popularized versions of the research which have been widely distributed in the media. For example, a magazine as ephemeral as *Vogue* featured an article which argued that "the woman's movement changed sexual politics; it was okay for the women to be the new sexual hunters and gatherers"; that "economically, men have been demystified"; and that "the culture right now is a peculiar, complicated, postfeminist, postmacho wasteland."[14] As Rosser notes, "We can never know whether or not there are real biological differences between males and females because we can never separate the biological from the environmental."[15] One does not have to be a feminist to query the value of a biological determinism which insists that biology defines behavior and that such biological effects as man-the-hunter may be studied separately from the effects of culture.[16]

III

Contemporary male writers have individually challenged the assumed biological relationship between aggression and male bonding. Rather than redefine the distribution of rewards, as Tiger hypothesizes as a possibility for social change, Frederick Busch, John Irving, and Larry Woiwode admit women to the bond. When imagined by these writers, women are not merely the source of rivalry but also the force of mediation. If the dividing line between territory and town is no longer as culturally demarcated as American novelists from Cooper to Dickey show it to be, then there can be no mythic space designated the special province of homosocial males.

One understands that the eradication of the always-beckoning frontier is an issue. Both Cooper and Dickey wrote their novels out of the urgency of this loss. The closing of the frontier—a thesis memorably argued by Frederick J. Turner a century ago—had not only cultural but literary reverberations: the bonded companions as American Adams had no place to go. With the constraint of time inhibiting the freedom of space, the Adam figure (rarely an Eve figure) had to fool himself or turn toward society and take a stand. The sound of the axes becomes as literal in the twentieth century as it was metaphorical in Cooper's day, and the Edenic promise of spaciousness degenerates to the containment of borders. The psychological shock is significant, for the Adamic hero and his male cohort are expelled from Eden. How can they light out for the territory when the territory is all used up? Faced with the disappearance of space, the bonded companions must now confront life where they find it. The result is a psychological shrinking, as illustrated in the contrast between Natty Bumppo and Lewis Medlock: Natty believes in possibility, but Lewis tries to avoid death. With the promise of possibility diminished, the complexities of life grab the advantage that the Adamic figure always assumed he had controlled. Men without women will no longer do. The confinement of the parlor and the contamination of sex, long the myths of exclusion for the masculine wilderness of the American novel, are now freed of their negative connotations. Women are everywhere.

Thus the issue in American novels today is broader than the disappearance of the frontier. One might point to Alaska as the mythical territory not yet eradicated but merely moved north instead of west (as in Mailer's *Why Are We in Vietnam?*). There in that huge state of natural splendor and open terrain, the argument would go, bonded males could join the ghost of Jack London and plunge into the adventure where women may not dare. (Significantly, James Dickey wrote a screenplay of London's *The Call of the Wild* that was produced for television.) But even the myth of Alaska as the final domain of the male prerogative has been exploded. In 1985 John Hawkes published *Adventures in the Alaskan Skin Trade*, a splendid intertextual combination of blood excitement by Jack London, tall tales by Mark Twain, and comic postmodernism by Hawkes.[17] Planting sex squarely in the wilderness, Hawkes creates a female narrator who controls both the text and the territory. More important, she controls the men who are foolish enough to try to emulate Leatherstocking's heroics in a land of snow and ice. Her comments about her father, which she makes from the middle of the wilderness, indicate her dismissal of males from Natty Bumppo through Nick Adams to Lewis Medlock: "But no matter the treachery of his innocence and misguided masculinity; no matter his Alaskan history of ever-increasing brutal flights of fancy . . . and no matter that his entire life was my seduction and betrayal" (92). No pristine male as innocent American Adam for her: Hawkes's female narrator equates Adamic innocence with misguided masculinity in a flippant tone that would shock the canonical American novelists. Thus she uses irony to make fun of the loyalty of male bonding that is at the heart of traditional American literature: "As for the bumper sticker on the jeep, it doesn't exactly represent my private views, isn't exactly true to me in the way 'Heed Hedonism' is. I'm *sworn to fun* as the bumper sticker says, but given my situation and my commitment to the Alaskan-Yukon Gamelands, I've been remarkably loyal to the men in my life" (93). Modernizing Cooper's Cora, Hawkes stresses his narrator's androgynous strength, gives her the voice that American novelists have historically denied women, and praises her sexuality.

The point is that Hawkes is not alone. Rather than only a postmodern master committed to outflanking the influential presence of the mythic novel of male privilege, the Hawkes of *Adventures in the Alaskan Skin Trade* is in the mainstream of the current tendency of male novelists to use women to mitigate male bonds. The loss of open territory—the very reason that Lewis Medlock and Ed Gentry hurry to the wild river—is one cause of the new direction in contemporary American fiction, and it is a loss that suggests a psychological diminishment for the male who would play Natty Bumppo today. But social pressure is another cause of change. Men still bond in American fiction, and aggression still spills over into violence, but women can no longer be relegated to the bedroom in good faith.

The new feminism and the perspicacity of feminist anthropology have formed a different social and psychological climate that contemporary male novelists have felt, however indirectly. Carolyn Heilbrun observes, "What has been lost sight of, I believe, are the feelings of individual men who have rejected the follies of male chauvinism and patriarchy, but are after all human beings with decades behind *them* who need some understanding of the struggles they are undergoing in a still unreformed society."[18] The issue is, of course, more than equal pay for equal work, or women in the boardroom. No matter their importance, these social pressures are merely cultural indicators of a more significant though obvious anthropological pressure: the equal value of men and women. The division of labor and the resulting hierarchy of gender formalized by the advent of group (male) hunting can no longer be accepted as an easily definable line of demarcation between the sexes. According to traditional American fiction, Cooper's dark-haired Cora and Dickey's model with the golden eye belong at home, engaged in what Marilynne Robinson would ironically call "housekeeping,"[19] but the new novelists of male bonding do not capitalize on the old literary equations of female and the kitchen, women and the snake, sexuality and the Fall. Although shrunken, there is still territory, and male writers still send bonded men into it. For Frederick Busch the mythic wilderness is upstate New York; for John Irving it is the large attic in an old house or even a stone quarry.

Women belong in the wilderness.

They have always belonged there.

In the American novel of the 1980s that is where they are.

Notes

1. Lionel Tiger, *Men in Groups* (New York: Random House, 1969).

2. Tim Carrigan, Bob Connell, and John Lee, "Hard and Heavy: Toward a New Sociology of Masculinity," *Beyond Patriarchy: Essays by Men on Pleasure, Power, and Change*, ed. Michael Kaufman (New York: Oxford University Press, 1987) 139–92.

3. Carmen Schifellite, "Beyond Tarzan and Jane Genes: Toward a Critique of Biological Determinism," *Beyond Patriarchy* 45–63.

4. Peter Schwenger, *Phallic Critiques: Masculinity and Twentieth-Century Literature* (London: Routledge and Kegan Paul, 1984).

5. Alison Wylie, Kathleen Okruhlik, Leslie Thielen-Wilson, and Sandra Morton, "Bibliography on Feminism and Science," *Women's Studies International Forum* 12 (1989): 379–88.

6. Ruth Bleier, *Science and Gender: A Critique of Biology and Its Theories on Women* (New York: Pergamon, 1984).

7. Edward O. Wilson, *Sociobiology: The New Synthesis* (Cambridge: Harvard University Press, 1975); see esp. 567–69.

8. In *On Human Nature* (Cambridge: Harvard University Press, 1978), Wilson defends himself against those (presumably including feminist anthropologists) whose "beliefs leave them no option but rejection": "The social sciences are still too young and weak, and evolutionary theory itself still too imperfect, for the propositions re-

viewed here to be carved in stone. It is my conviction nevertheless that the existing evidence favors them and through them the broader confidence in biological inquiry that forms the main thrust of this exposition" (x–xi).

9. Ruth Bleier, "Myths of the Biological Inferiority of Women: An Exploration of the Sociology of Biological Research," *University of Michigan Papers in Women's Studies* 2 (1976): 40–41.

10. Adrienne Zihlman and Nancy Tanner, "Women in Evolution: Part I," *Signs* 1 (1976): 585–608; "Part II," *Signs* 4 (1978): 4–20.

11. For an overview of the more recent debates in anthropology, see Sherry B. Ortner, "Theory in Anthropology since the Sixties," *Comparative Studies in Society and History* 26 (Jan. 1984): 126–66.

12. Sally Slocum, "Woman the Gatherer: Male Bias in Anthropology," *Toward an Anthropology of Women*, ed. Rayna R. Reiter (New York: Monthly Review Press, 1975) 39.

13. Donna J. Haraway, "In the Beginning Was the Word: The Genesis of Biological Theory," *Signs* 6 (1984): 477.

14. Barbara Lippert, "Send in the Wimps," *Vogue* (Nov. 1988): 414, 456.

15. Sue V. Rosser, "Good Science: Can It Ever Be Gender Free?" *Women's Studies International Forum* 11 (1988): 17.

16. Marian Lowe is blunter: As a serious theory, sociobiology is not scientific but political. This is because sociobiologists argue that, since biological factors shape society, one should not tamper with the status quo. To do so would be to "go against nature." As Lowe points out, popular support for biological determinist theories normally coincide with periods of social questioning because those who resist change may then use science as the rationale for maintaining the status quo. See Lowe, "Sociobiology and Sex Differences," *Signs* 4 (1978): 118–25.

17. John Hawkes, *Adventures in the Alaskan Skin Trade* (New York: Simon and Schuster, 1985).

18. Carolyn Heilbrun, "Millet's Sexual Politics: A Year Later," *Aphra* 2 (Summer 1971) 44.

19. Marilynne Robinson, *Housekeeping* (New York: Farrar, Straus, & Giroux, 1981).

Chapter Four

Women Enter the Wilderness

Frederick Busch: *Sometimes I Live in the Country*

Frederick Busch's aggressive males are father and son, and they bond in *Sometimes I Live in the Country* (1986), a novel written in a style that consciously recalls Hemingway: the simple vocabulary, the short sentences, the repetition.[1] The diction and prose rhythms reflect those of a thirteen-year-old boy no longer a child of grammar school but not yet an adolescent in easy sight of maturity. Reading *Sometimes I Live in the Country*, one thinks of Huck Finn or Nick Adams. Yet the allusions to Twain and Hemingway are ironic, for Busch deliberately deconstructs their ideal of men without women, a world where male bonding more than suffices except when sexual needs intervene. Hemingway's Nick Adams spends much of his time trying simultaneously to learn about sex and to avoid women, but Busch's Petey knows that his equilibrium is irrevocably disrupted when he is hauled off to the wilderness by a father who is in flight from the wife and mother.

Busch's wilderness is upstate New York, not Cooper's endless forest or even Dickey's wild river, but an open territory nonetheless, especially for someone like Petey, who has been raised in the teeming crowds of Brooklyn. The irony is that the territory is no longer inviting. The possibilities in Cooper for a new Eden or in Dickey for the old trials of manhood are reduced by Busch to the elemental level of sheer survival. Petey's father, "Pop," plays Chingachgook to his son's Uncas in an effort to reassert the traditional myth of the American novel that bars women from the homosocial unity of bonded males, but Busch knows that American culture has changed so radically that Cooper's—and Dickey's—myth will no longer suffice. Thus he begins *Sometimes I Live in the Country* where Cooper ends *The Last of the Mohicans:* with the possibility of the death of the son.

Petey forces his father's pistol into his mouth and pulls the trigger. The allusion to Hemingway's suicide is clear. That the gun misfires does not negate the shock of the scene, for the violent death of the son is a blatant challenge to the efficacy of the male bond. Cooper eliminates Uncas for reasons discussed earlier, but he may do so without undermining the masculine wilderness because Uncas is finally extraneous to the homosocial brotherhood of Natty and Chingachgook. Similarly, Dickey may destroy Drew, who is, like Uncas, the best man in the group, because Dickey, like his forerunner Cooper, has constructed his novel so that the focus of the bond falls on two other men. Busch does not permit that luxury because he refuses to accept the myth. Deliberately casting *Sometimes I Live in the Country* in the guise of the American novel of men without women, he explodes the myth in two ways. First, *both* Petey and Pop must survive if male bonding is to have any legitimacy at all; second, in order to survive they need a female to cement the bond.

Sometimes I Live in the Country is thus not only fine fiction but also evidence of a significant change in American novels written by white, middle-class males. Busch does not pontificate, for he uses wry humor throughout: "The sky sat on top of their hill. He was in between the grass and the black air and the stars. Pop's gun was black too and it was colder than the ground. It filled his mouth. It was a small barrel but it filled his mouth up. He gagged on the gun that stuffed his tongue up into his head. He decided to close his eyes. Then he opened them. He didn't want to miss anything" (3). It is clear from the opening page that Petey's position between stars and grass signals more a predicament of alienation than a potential for Eden. The boy's physical displacement from the city, the very domain that Cooper, Melville, Twain, Hemingway, and Dickey hope to escape, illustrates his psychological displacement from life. If Petey is to live, he must be near women and the society that they represent.

This is a startling development in American fiction, one that many readers are unprepared for when they pick up contemporary novels such as *Sometime I Live in the Country*. Isolated from the female, the aggressive male now seeks to kill not the threats to male bonding, as in Cooper and Dickey, but himself. D. H. Lawrence's terms "hard, stoic, isolate, and a killer" still apply to the American literary hero in varying degrees, but Busch knows that the circumstances of culture have changed. The immaculate wilderness of upstate New York, the territory that Cooper mythologized in *Mohicans*, is now a burnt-out landscape populated with people whom Petey dismisses as "cornheads." They live in trailers and use outhouses and batten down their roofs with tires. Poor, uneducated, and bigoted, they are Cooper's enemy Indians without Magua's nobility. Petey has a Chingachgook to guide him, for his father is a former cop, "a tough-ass" with heavy neck and belly and the strength to lift another person off the ground. Yet Busch's combination of Chingachgook and Leatherstocking in the late twentieth century crosses the border with his male companion not to step toward myth but to run from law. Divorcing his wife and demanding his son, Pop violates the very statutes he is sworn to observe when he snatches Petey out of Brooklyn and hides him in the land of the cornheads. Busch's allusions are unforced, but he encourages readers to hear echoes of the debate in *The Prairie* when Natty Bumppo and Ishmael Bush argue the conflict between the needs of the individual and the requirements of law. The significant difference is Pop's lack of the moral authority that—as with Natty—always confers mythic stature. American culture no longer nurtures the ideal except as a nostalgic recognition of an opportunity forever lost. At the very beginning of *Sometimes I Live in the Country*, then, Busch poses a question that speaks to both traditional American fiction and contemporary American society: How can a man play Leatherstocking–Chingachgook and try to escape the civilization that women represent when women are finally in the wilderness where they, too, belong?

In other words, Pop accepts the role of the American literary hero that Cooper defined and Dickey sustains, but Petey is Busch's representative of a newer generation of males who will not relegate women to secondary status. The bonding between Petey and Pop is firm, but the father underestimates the effect on the son of separation from the mother. The violation of what Mary D. Salter Ainsworth calls "attachments" and Lionel Tiger and Robin Fox call the mother-child bond precipitates the crisis in the male homosocial bond. Thus Busch creates Lizzie Bean—Miz Bean—as surrogate mother and wife, and then varies the pattern of male rivalry described by Eve Kosofsky Sedgwick and René Girard. Ainsworth observes, "Despite the rich testimony from history and literature that fathers can have strong commitments to their offspring, the tendency has been to consider the bond of father to child as somehow less deeply rooted than the bond of mother to child."[2] During the past decade, however, research in psychology and anthropology suggests that fathers can and do engage in a care-giving role that results in bonding. Male nurturing occurs, argues Ainsworth, when the father has "sufficient exposure" to the child. Busch takes these ideas, removes a boy from attachment bonds with mother and peers, and examines what happens when an adolescent male must nurture a new bond with an adult male. Interestingly, Busch conceived *Sometimes I Live in the Country* with not only the threatened suicide of the male in mind but also the mitigating power of the female, Lizzie Bean.

The most important character in *Sometimes I Live in the Country*, Miz Bean was first introduced in Busch's earlier novel *Rounds* (1979).[3] In that sensitive novel of physicians and pain Lizzie is a psychologist and unwed mother who is persuaded by the pediatrician Dr. Silver to put her baby up for adoption. Silver has already failed his wife and son, and he thinks he has given Lizzie the correct advice. But he betrays her when he takes her for a mistress. Though a woman of intelligence and insight, Lizzie is left at the end of *Rounds* with nobody, utterly alone in the middle of a supermarket. Within a year of the publication of *Rounds*, Busch was curious about her fate: "I didn't do justice by her. I'd like to write a whole book about her some day. . . . She was a victim of Dr. Silver. He used her and she knew it. He didn't deserve her, though he needed her."[4] *Sometimes I Live in the Country* is Busch's "whole book" about Lizzie Bean, a novel in which her loss of the adopted child reflects Petey's loss of the biological mother.

In lesser hands the domestic particulars of the crisis in *Sometimes I Live in the Country* could degenerate to sentimentality, to a saccharine celebration of women, but Busch avoids the exploitation of emotion by letting Petey's sardonic voice direct the text. More important, he questions two primary conclusions of social scientists who have probed the phenomenon of male bonding: that men derive significant satisfactions from homosocial bonds that they cannot receive from male-female attachments, and that men consciously exclude women from these bonds. Thus while Busch deliberately gives Petey a brash voice intended to recall Huck Finn or Nick Adams, he consciously undermines the notion of the masculine wilderness. Writing within the tradition in order to deconstruct it, he encourages the reader to remember Nick Adams's naïve confidence in "Indian Camp" that "he would never die" when Petey is introduced while forcing a pistol into his mouth. The contrast with the tradition is both fearful and startling. Busch acknowledges the heritage of Cooper, Hemingway, and Dickey and then shows that men-without-women is a dead end, that only a female—Lizzie Bean—can pull Petey out of despair.

Like most males Petey sees primarily the exterior when he looks at a woman. His initial description of Miz Bean, couched in Hemingwayesque prose rhythms, suggests how far he has to go to break with the tradition and admit women to the unit of male bonding: "She was tall but Pop was taller. But she was tall and she had big shoulders. She had a long nose. She wasn't like a model on TV" (5). Neither Cooper's raven-haired Cora nor Dickey's golden-eyed beauty queen, Lizzie is a woman of reality who has already staked out her claim in the woods. She is the head guidance counselor at Petey's school "and the one you had to talk to about your life" (7). After he learns not to make snide remarks about the sisters of his peers, as if gender jokes were a male prerogative, Petey arranges a talk about life with Miz Bean.

Cooper, Hemingway, and Dickey begin with the assumption that Cora, Prudie, and the model are sexual totems who must remain in the home if they want to protect their sexuality. When female beauty threatens male bonds, males will respond aggressively. Busch's skill at challenging the long heritage of effaced women in American fiction is evident when he shows that Petey is curious about female anatomy, as any heterosexual male would be, and yet senses that sex is not the measure of a woman. One of his teachers may have "a body like *Penthouse*," and Petey may despair about sex that "nobody told them where to put what; . . . he had heard there were a lot of places to get lost down there" (7), but his need for Miz Bean does not undercut his masculinity to the extent that either he or Lizzie has to die. Indeed, Busch celebrates simultaneously Lizzie's femininity and her androgyny. Tall with big nose and long feet, she has Pop and Petey dreaming of her, learning that *their* survival depends on her presence in the territory beyond Brooklyn.

The gender relationships in *Sometimes I Live in the Country* are convincing because Busch refuses to pretend that gender stereotypes do not exist. A similar novel written for political persuasion or gender propaganda would either attack the stereotypes or ignore them. Busch, however, recognizes their prominence, describes them honestly as part of his characterization of the bonded males, and then works through them to show that the inclusion of women enhances rather than dilutes the male bond. This is why Petey and Pop often seem two sides of the same coin. Living in the territory, they form a male society of two, just as Natty and Chingachgook did in the same location a century and a half earlier: "They talked about each other to each other sometimes when things were good in the house and no one was shouting. They trusted each other sometimes" (11). But unlike Leatherstocking and Chingachgook, they acknowledge the company of women in the league of gentlemen. All they have to do is get beyond the stereotypes hyped by a media-conscious culture that defines the ideal woman according to her proximity to *Penthouse*. As Petey thinks about "all those tits," so Pop watches television programs featuring "cops, fast cars, girls in tight clothes with big behinds" (9,12).

Although Petey mistakenly believes that his mother has deserted him, when the truth is that his father has lit out for the territory in traditional American fashion to escape the restrictions of a woman-ruled home, matriarchy and patriarchy are not the issues here. Busch's irony is that women already occupy Pop's escape route. Busch dismisses as a false dilemma the culturally tested tradition that bonded males must choose between matriarchy (Cooper's Alice) or dream-women with "big behinds" (Dickey's model), and he argues that female sexuality and male strength can be combined in a woman like Miz Bean. All Pop and Petey have to do is accept the radical cultural change that inviting her into the bond would entail. Aware of the influence that the novel of masculine mythology has in American society, Busch indirectly suggests how difficult the invitation will be when he designates Petey's favorite novel as Louis L'Amour's *Hondo*, a descendant of the Leatherstocking tales and a fiction with "the tough man sleeping outside with his dog named Dog to protect the kid and his mother" (16). To sleep in a bed with a woman would be a confession of weakness. Pop's cops-and-robbers television shows are of the same genre.

Eve Sedgwick's thesis of the homosocial bond being solidified when two males become rivals for the same female is pertinent to the crisis in *Sometimes I Live in the Country*. An updated version of Cooper's bad Indians attacks in the guise of the Ku Klux Klan, and his Magua minus courage and pathos appears as the despicable yet dangerous Reverend Staynes, but Busch brings a needed variation to the tradition when he lets the already bonded males vie for a reprise of an androgynous Cora. Unlike Cooper, the question he asks is not how to get rid of her but how to accommodate her. Pop needs a lover and Petey needs a mom. The issue for Lizzie—and it is an issue that is not developed in the canonical American novel—is whether she is willing to accept their burdens. Natty and Chingachgook, Ishmael and Queequeg, Huck and Jim, and Ed Gentry and Lewis Medlock are not permitted to carry such gender predicaments with them into the territory. Little wonder, then, that Petey thinks, "they were in a new country" (25).

Discrimination against women, be it in American culture or American fiction, forms the basis of a second civil rights movement. Thus Busch constructs the surface plot of *Sometimes I Live in the Coun-*

try around Pop and Petey's search for the heritage of the black residents of upstate New York. The progress of their quest reflects the growth of their awareness of Lizzie's importance in their lives, and their embrace of black Mr. O'Nolan and female Miz Bean signifies an advance in American society. While on the quest, Petey wonders if they have crossed the border to the domain of science fiction movies like *The Land That Time Forgot*. In many ways he is correct, for the country that they find is not the culture that he lost in Brooklyn.

In the land of the cornheads, as one bigoted resident explains, "You might count Injuns as coloreds" (39–40). The echo of Cooper is clear. So are the echoes of Hemingway's insistence in the Nick Adams stories that Indians are different, or Dickey's distinction between the bonded males from Atlanta and the predators from North Georgia. The point is that the American novel of male mythology normally designates an Other as the threat to be surmounted in order to prove the superiority of masculinity. Busch understands that the exclusion of blacks or Native Americans is a metaphor for the avoidance of women. This is why Petey must grow out of his prejudice against country folk before he can accept Miz Bean as more than a rival for his father's affection. "Miz Bean," he learns to say. "You don't say Miss anymore. It's chauvinist" (54). This is also why Lizzie, and not a male descendant of Natty Bumppo, defines the truth behind the male quest for the fugitive black people of the territory: "You're looking for something you can't find. Which could mean that you don't want to find the *other* thing—which you're *really* looking for" (63). The "other" thing is women. Admitting their loss, but reluctant to break with the cultural heritage of males in the wilderness, the two men attempt to balance the weight of absence-as-presence by substituting the search for blacks for the need of women. As Pop says, "Everybody always has to deal with absent things" (63).

Unlike his forerunners in the canonical American novel, Busch insists that the exclusion of Cora or Lizzie creates an absence at the heart of the nation. On the literal level the wife and mother is missing from *Sometimes I Live in the Country*, but on the metaphorical level the loss of the woman means the dissolution of family, the breakdown of community, and the weakening of culture. The United States of the 1980s will no longer support Cooper's ideal of the 1820s. For Busch this reordering of priorities in response to both feminist pressure and revaluation of a male literary myth results in the neutralization of the long-established binary opposition of masculine and Other. Male bonding still holds, as anthropologists have demonstrated that it always will, but Busch insists that recognition of the female does not mean emasculation of the male.

The emotional center of *Sometimes I Live in the Country* is, then, not the "big" scene in which Petey-as-Uncas stands off the Klansmen-as-Indians but the exchange between Petey and Miz Bean when Lizzie offers him the gift of her deepest secret. She tells him about the moment in *Rounds* when she gave up her baby for adoption. When Petey hopes that he may be her lost child, he takes the first step toward accepting Lizzie's rightful place in the forest. Busch thus rejects the long-established notion in American literature that female sexuality compromises male idealism. Miz Bean's androgyny recalls Cora's strength, but Busch, unlike Cooper, refuses to equate passionate women with the crawling serpent in Eden. The fort that Petey builds and the castle that he draws in art class are metaphors for the masculine habitats of American mythology within which men may no longer hide. Immediately following Lizzie's revelation to Petey, Busch provides an indirect contrast between *Sometimes I Live in the Country* and *The Deerslayer* when he describes Pop and Petey angrily listening to the exploding rifles of deer season and watching two Klansmen drag a dead deer across their land. Natty Bumppo disappears when Cora remains in the wilderness. Given the choice between Leatherstocking and Lizzie, Busch's bonded males will choose the latter every time.

Aware that Pop and Petey are more like brothers than parent and child, Miz Bean is the emotional cohesion for a radical renovation of American fiction: a homosocial relationship that welcomes not only women but blacks. When Mr. O'Nolan, the retired black teacher, joins Miz Bean as another surrogate parent for Petey, Busch completes the multigender, multiracial social unit that Cooper contemplated in *The Last of the Mohicans* and then denied in favor of the immaculate friendship of pristine men. Not masculine mythology but the American family is Mr. O'Nolan's teaching specialty, and the family that they form together out of the richly varied strands of the national culture turns out to be strong enough to repudiate the reactionary Klan. Faithful to the American literary heritage, male novelists from Cooper through Dickey either kill off those who would plant a family in the wilderness or send them back to the settlement. As Petey asks, "Or is prejudice just part of American history? I was thinking—what the settlers, the colonists said about how evil the Indians were. It kind of sounded like the Klan, you know?" (139). Sadly, his query is an *American* question. It shapes a tradition that flouts the ideals of the nation. Busch bucks that tradition.

John Irving: *A Prayer for Owen Meany*

Where Frederick Busch alludes to Cooper in his novel of male bonding, John Irving draws on Cooper and Hawthorne. Both *Sometimes I Live in the Country* and *A Prayer for Owen Meany* (1989) celebrate women as the glue that guarantees the bond—of father and son in the former novel, of boyhood friends in the latter—and both authors acknowledge the long legacy of the canonical American novel and the current need to rethink its assumptions.[5] But while Busch's nod to Cooper is indirect, Irving's bow to Hawthorne is explicit: the central female character in *A Prayer for Owen Meany* is named Hester.

"We'll talk about Hester in our graves!" says John Wheelwright in the middle of Irving's long novel (372), and thus points the reader to *The Scarlet Letter* as the first great American tale of sexual transgression and religious doubt. Hester indeed haunts the American psyche. As the passionate woman banished by the governing patriarchy, she is the exemplar in American literature of the female living on the edges of society, positioned in the clearing between the forest and the town. Forced to hide her sexuality when among the men *and* women who condemn her, Hester is free to let down her hair when she crosses the clearing to enter the dark woods. But while she ostensibly accepts her culture's definition of femininity, she never repents. Always the rebel and thus forever the heroine, Hester uses adultery as a catalyst for creativity. Dimmesdale merely wastes away.

The minister represents the town while Mistress Hibbins is at ease in the forest. Only Hester has commerce with both. The challenge to religious faith that Dimmesdale suffers in the woods is a crucial issue not only for *The Scarlet Letter* but also for American fiction, for Hawthorne clearly questions the notion of the endless wilderness as the domain of the new American Eden. Unlike Cooper's infinite expanse, Hawthorne's forest is defined by what Melville called "the blackness of darkness." Hester is Hawthorne's female Natty Bumppo, the woman who momentarily leaves society to escape the very institutions that plague Leatherstocking: a restrictive church and a punitive law. But where Natty has the psychological and physical support of his bonded companion Chingachgook, Hester's potential bond fails her. Dimmesdale cannot survive in the wilderness. Twice he crosses the clearing, and twice he returns with his faith shaken: the first time as an adulterer, the second as a blasphemer. His Election Day Sermon is the message of a hypocrite.[6]

John Irving is very much aware of the separation of the sexes in the traditional American novel, as well as the religious connotations of the American wilderness. The epigraphs to *A Prayer for Owen Meany*, particularly those from Paul's letter to the Philippians and from Frederick Buechner, emphasize the tension between faith and doubt, and his public comments on the novel stress the heroism of the person who would believe: " 'I'm moved and impressed by people with a great deal of religious faith,' says Irving, an Episcopalian who admits that the compulsory churchgoing of his youth has had a cumulative effect. But, he adds, 'the Christ story impresses me in heroic, not religious, terms.' "[7] Owen Meany is Irving's re-creation of Dimmesdale, but as a heroic believer who is strong where Dimmesdale is weak, courageous where Dimmesdale is cowardly. Loving Hester while simultaneously fostering the male bond with his boyhood friend John Wheelwright, Meany personifies Irving's challenge to such anthropologists as Lionel Tiger who argue that women dilute bonding.

Reading the opening pages of *A Prayer for Owen Meany*, one might think that Irving had decided to accept the paradigm of the canonical American novel. As he concedes, "I follow the form of the 19th-century novel; that was the century which produced the models of the form. I'm old-fashioned, a storyteller."[8] Yet Irving's traditional form shapes an untraditional theme that suggests a different view of male bonding: John Wheelwright, the narrator, informs the reader that Meany has killed Wheelwright's mother. What better way to guarantee the homosocial bond than to eliminate the literal presence of matriarchy? With mothers dead and Hesters banished, men have no need to follow Natty and Chingachgook into the wilderness. But such is not the case in *Owen Meany*. For as Wheelwright makes clear, *his* Dimmesdale's faith is strong enough to convert him too: "I am doomed to remember a boy with a wrecked voice—not because of his voice, or because he was the smallest person I ever knew, or even because he was the instrument of my mother's death, but because he is the reason I believe in God" (13). Of Puritan ancestry as diluted as Hawthorne's was in his day, John Wheelwright rewrites *The Scarlet Letter* from his newly found territory of Canada.[9] He literally crosses the border to tell the tale. Yet his focus is primarily on the various American wildernesses that define his bond with Owen Meany. Irving comments: "Even if you try hard to look away from the U.S., it is there in your face like a flag."[10]

The section of the United States that Wheelwright recalls is appropriately named Gravesend. Although a real town in New Hampshire, Gravesend is mythologized in *A Prayer for Owen Meany* as a locale that can accommodate male bonding without denying female presence. Gravesend is north of Boston, beyond the civilization of the supposed center of New England, and thus the proper territory for the social experiment of women in the bond. Reading of Hester's romp through Irving's New Hampshire, one remembers that Hawthorne's Massachusetts punished Hester Prynne. Like Frederick Busch, Irving does not shrink from the cultural implications of his tale. This is why Wheelwright's goal is to re-present the new American Eden, to rediscover an endless territory where Hesters are at ease and male bonding is forever. Residing in Canada, but writing of the United States, Wheelwright is the virgin male, the avoider of wombs, the symbolic brother of Owen Meany. In this sense, then, Wheelwright and Owen are Natty and Chingachgook, or even Lewis Medlock and Ed Gentry, but with this difference: Irving's pristine males, the one a virgin and the other a saint, do not feel threatened by women in the wilderness. What Wheelwright would like to do is not force Hester back to Boston but reimagine the mythic potential of America:

> For a moment, until the crows commence their harsh bickering, I can imagine that here, on Georgian Bay, I have found what was once called The New World—all over again, I have stumbled ashore on the undamaged land that Watahantowet sold to my ancestor. For in Georgian Bay it is possible to imagine North America as it was—before the United States began the murderous deceptions and the unthinking carelessness that have all but *spoiled* it! (376).

For all his nostalgia about the green promise of the new world, John Wheelwright is no Jay Gatsby trying to repeat the past. By the time he narrates his story, he has lost both his best friend and his mother. Dressing in white, as does Fitzgerald's Daisy, but accenting her outfit with red, as does Hawthorne's Hester, Wheelwright's mother combines the maternal and the erotic. Accidentally killed by Owen Meany when the boys are eleven years old, she is Cooper's Cora and Alice Munro united, a sexy matriarch who, like Hester, refuses to identify the father of her child:

> She was even a sweater girl in the summer, because she favored those summer-weight jersey dresses; she had a nice tan, and the dress was a simple, white-cotton one—clinging about the bosom and waist, full skirt below—and she wore a red scarf to hold her hair up, off her bare shoulders. . . . Everyone was always staring at my mother (39).

Her absurd death—she is struck by a baseball—frees the boys from the supposed restrictions of matriarchy and opens their lives to Hester, the archetypal dark lady of American fiction.

Although John and Owen create an icon from the mother's dress, it is significant that they do not bond until the matriarch dies. Even at this point in *A Prayer for Owen Meany* one might expect Irving to follow the paradigm of the traditional American novel. The homosocial affinity takes place only when the personification of society's inhibitions is eliminated, and the inadvertent perpetrator of the disaster is a childlike version of D. H. Lawrence's summation of the American literary hero—hard, isolate, stoic, and a killer. After the death of the erotic mother the bonded males listen not for Indian war cries but for the crack of a baseball bat, an unexpected source of violence:

> I know many people, today, who instinctively cringe at any noise even faintly resembling a gunshot or an exploding bomb—a car backfires, the handle of a broom or a shovel *whacks* flat against a cement or a linoleum floor, a kid detonates a firecracker in an empty trash can, and my friends cover their heads, primed (as we all are, today) for the terrorist attack or the random assassin. But not me; and never Owen Meany. . . . Owen Meany and I were permanently conditioned to flinch at the sound of a different kind of gunshot: that much-loved and most American sound of summer, the good old crack of the bat! (82).

The absurdity of the tragedy is Irving's sign to the reader that the pattern of the canon will not direct *A Prayer for Owen Meany*. When the bonded companions light out for the territory after the lamented but liberating elimination of the mother figure, they find a wilderness despite the shrinking of the American Eden. Ironically, they locate it in the grandmother's attic. There, amid vast and mysterious shelves of old clothes and discarded shoes, sharp angles and forbidding corners, John and Owen confront in the guise of a stuffed armadillo the reduced circumstances of Leatherstocking's deer or Ahab's whale or Ike McCaslin's bear. Irving's ironic allusion to the mythic exploits of past American literary heroes undercuts any lingering notion that the traditional novel is significant today. The stuffed armadillo is "like some relic of the animal world, some throwback to an age when men were taking a risk every time they left the cave" (54). Despite anthropological hypotheses, Irving's males do not bond to engage in the tribal hunt. The allusions to Cooper become comically pointed when Irving names the neighborhood dog Sagamore, after Leatherstocking's nickname for Chingachgook in *The Last of the Mohicans*. Now dead, and thus recalling Natty's stuffed dog at the conclusion of *The Prairie*, Sagamore illustrates the watering down of the American literary myth. The dilution is complete when the heritage of the great chief Chingachgook is exchanged for a crushed dog and a stuffed armadillo that is missing its claws.

Irving's revision of the American novel has political implications, for he uses Wheelwright's residency in Canada as a perspective from which to criticize the United States now that the retreating wilderness has lost out to the sound of the axes. The likelihood of that loss was memorably foreshadowed in the debates between Natty Bumppo and Ishmael Bush in *The Prairie*, but at least the ideal of the national dream of Edenic territory remained vibrant in 1827. For Irving's bonded males, however, idyllic myth degenerates into bungling politics. Wheelwright's despair over Ronald Reagan's presidency suggests that the political discussions of Natty and Ishmael have declined into the public antagonisms of a leaderless nation. From the Great Serpent Chingachgook to the Great Communicator Reagan and a stuffed armadillo is a culturally significant fall. Rather than accept his place in Leatherstocking's legacy and lament what he sees while defending the myth of the country, Wheelwright flees the culture to debunk the dream: "Americans should be forced to see how *ridiculous* they appear to the rest of the world! They should listen to someone else's version of themselves—to *anyone else's* version!" (203).

The point is that much of the new version comes from the perspective of women. For all the references to the political undercurrents in the Leatherstocking saga, Irving's most important re-creation of the text of the American novel is his rethinking of the feminine role. In *The World According to Garp* (1978) he satirizes the militant Ellen Jamesians, sympathizes with the original Ellen James, and laughs at Jenny's efforts to blame all worldly ills on males and sex, but his characterization of Hester in *A Prayer for Owen Meany* is more serious. The bonded males must revaluate their position when the masculine wilderness of the grandmother's attic is invaded not by a devious Ishmael Bush or encroaching settlers but by a woman. The sound of the ax becomes the curve of a breast when Hester walks into the attic. Significantly, the modern Hester is not about to wear an A.

Rather than direct her creative energies to the sewing needle, Irving's Hester rips the threads from her blouse. She has just become an adolescent when she first meets Owen Meany, but her kinship with her voluptuous ancestor is already evident:

> In her T-shirt, there was little doubt that she would one day have an impressive bosom; its early blossoming was as apparent as her manly biceps. And the way she tore the thread out of her damaged blouse with her teeth—snarling and cursing in the process, as if she were

eating her blouse—must have demonstrated to Owen the full potential
of Hester's dangerous mouth; at that moment, her basic rapaciousness
was quite generously displayed (70).

This is a Hester who does not hide her sexuality, who does not play
by the boys' rules, and who does not bend to a New England concept of the proper role of women. When she walks beyond the formal
living room to enter the unkempt attic, she effectively stakes her
claim to a domain that has previously been the playing field of males.
Dubbed Hester the Molester by the boys who are in awe of the creative force of her femininity, she is the initiator, the sexual aggressor
in the wilderness of the male hideaway.

Irving consciously unifies the allusions to Hawthorne and Cooper when he describes Hester's initial meeting with Owen in the attic. Greeting Hester as if he were a kind of otherworldly companion,
Owen appears as nothing so simple as another tribe or race but as a
being from another realm, Christlike, beyond the human. His en-
trance is a delightful parody of Natty Bumppo's introduction in *The
Prairie*, except, of course, that Leatherstocking is an old man while
Owen is a boy:

> "The powerful morning sun struck Owen's head from above, and from
> a little behind him, so that the light itself seemed to be presenting
> him. . . . With his hands clasped behind his back, he looked as arm-
> less as Watahantowet, and in that blaze of sunlight he looked like a
> gnome plucked fresh from a fire, with his ears still aflame. . . . A tiny
> but fiery god, sent to adjudicate the errors of our ways (71).

Only in the postfeminist American novel may Hester Prynne meet
Natty Bumppo on equal terms. The most famous woman in American
fiction—an adulteress, an artist figure, and a healer—salutes the
most archetypal male in American literature—a virgin, a solitary, and
a killer.

Irving understands that adolescent willingness to transcend traditional barriers does not necessarily apply to parents. Steeped in the
lessons of American culture, which teach that males achieve manhood through bonding in a domain untainted by women, the guard-
ians of Owen and Wheelwright's society insist on separate educations
for Hester and the boys. Sexually aggressive Hester must be sent off
to school because Gravesend Academy, where Owen and John matric-
ulate, will not admit females. Once Hester invades the attic, prep
school becomes the new wilderness, the fallback retreat that offers
escape from the lure of female temptation. There, amid the rituals of
manhood, American males may earn the rewards of bonding. But as

Irving makes clear, women have similar needs that cannot be success-
fully displaced by such domestic activities as sewing and child care:
"Hester was in as much need of rescuing from the wildness within
her—and from the rural, north country rituals of *her* sex" (239).

Like Hester Prynne and Cora Munro before her, Hester tres-
passes the masculine wilderness with the power of sexuality, but unlike Hawthorne and Cooper, Irving does not punish her for what
Owen comically dubs "THE LUST CONNECTION." Determined
to avenge herself on the parents for treating her "like a girl," she
reverses the teaching process and educates the adults "regarding the
errors of their ways" (249). In other words, she rejects gender stereotypes, insists on her right to the territory beyond the parlor, and refuses to accept the A. Thus her second invasion of the masculine
province is her authoritative presence at the senior dance, where the
bonded males watch in admiration. Indeed, her body, the one element that adults cannot control, is now so expressive and thus so
threatening to the faculty chaperones and their wives that John
Wheelwright imagines her in a jungle; in, that is, the wilderness:

> For the Senior Dance, she wore a short black dress with spaghetti
> straps as thin as string; the dress had a full skirt, a fitted waist, and a
> deeply plunging neckline that exposed a broad expanse of Hester's
> throat and chest. . . . She wore no stockings and danced barefoot;
> around one ankle was a black rawhide thong. . . . We were all en-
> thralled. When Owen Meany danced with Hester, the sharp bridge of
> his nose fit perfectly in her cleavage; no one even "cut in" (263).

A short Natty Bumppo dances with a voluptuous Hester Prynne, and
their ensuing love affair signals a change in the understanding of gender in American fiction.

Irving solidifies his radical rewriting of the American novel when
he offers as the symbolic personification of the nation not Leatherstocking and Chingachgook, or Ishmael and Queequeg, or Huck and
Jim, or Nick Carraway and Gatsby, or Ike McCaslin and Sam Fathers,
but Hester and Marilyn Monroe. America perverts the promise of
these women just as it trashes its own ideals. But rather than the
nostalgia of the traditional novelist for the dream lost by the corruption of Edenic potential, Irving shows anger. The denial of women
results in the depletion of culture. As Owen Meany proclaims in capital letters, Marilyn Monroe's suicide—and by extension Cora's death
and Hester's punishment—affects everyone: "IT HAS TO DO
WITH *ALL* OF US. . . . SHE WAS JUST LIKE OUR WHOLE
COUNTRY—NOT QUITE YOUNG ANYMORE, BUT NOT OLD

EITHER. . . . AND SHE WAS LOOKING FOR SOMETHING—
I THINK SHE WANTED TO BE GOOD. . . . AND SHE WAS
VULNERABLE, TOO. SHE WAS NEVER QUITE HAPPY, SHE
WAS ALWAYS A LITTLE OVERWEIGHT. SHE WAS JUST
LIKE OUR WHOLE COUNTRY" (381). Owen argues—with, one
suspects, Irving's approval—that males stepped into the wilderness
of the New World and sullied what Fitzgerald eloquently described
as "the last and greatest of all human dreams; for a transitory en-
chanted moment man must have held his breath in the presence of
this continent, compelled into an aesthetic contemplation he neither
understood nor desired, face to face for the last time in history with
something commensurate to his capacity for wonder."[11] But the wonder turned to greed, and the greed turned to power, as Natty foresaw
in Ishmael Bush and as Owen Meany sees in the causes of Marilyn
Monroe's death: "THAT'S WHAT POWERFUL MEN DO TO
THIS COUNTRY—IT'S A BEAUTIFUL, SEXY, BREATHLESS
COUNTRY, AND POWERFUL MEN USE IT TO TREAT
THEMSELVES TO A THRILL! THEY SAY THEY LOVE IT
BUT THEY DON'T MEAN IT. THEY SAY THINGS TO MAKE
THEMSELVES APPEAR GOOD. [MARILYN] GOT USED, SHE
WAS USED *UP*. JUST LIKE THE COUNTRY" (381–82).

Anger over the results of the traditional male prerogative is why
Irving juxtaposes Owen's account of Marilyn Monroe's suicide with
Ronald Reagan's lies about the arms-for-hostage deal. One may or
may not approve of the political asides in *A Prayer for Owen Meany*,
but the point remains that Irving ties the heritage of culture to the
duplicity of politics. Both "use up" women and the country. Irving's
joke is that the contemporary Hester becomes a video rock star in
defiance of those who would keep her in the home. Taking the name
Hester the Molester for her act, and flaunting herself as "a fading
queen of the grittiest and randiest sort of rock 'n' roll," she insists on
the decline of America when she splices her rock videos with docu-
mentary footage from the Vietnam war (452). One need hardly stress
that Vietnam was the most recent national adventure of homosocial
males bonding against an alien tribe.

Like Hester Prynne, who turns prejudice and punishment into
art while challenging the male power of governors, jailers, and minis-
ters, so Irving's Hester assumes a religious aura in her creativity. But
where Hawthorne is affirmative in equating the A and the angel, Irving is pessimistic in joining the Molester and the Madonna. Writing
in 1850, Hawthorne still has hope that the American masculine wilderness may be tempered; writing a century and a half later, Irving is

not so sure. His Madonna is obviously a parody of the popular enter-
tainer of the 1980s who mixes rock music and religious symbols; but
in making Hester's props crucifixes, Irving also nudges the reader to
see her as a serious re-creation of the Mother of God in a fallen
Eden. Her love for the Christ-figure Owen Meany is her redemption.
Unlike Dimmesdale, the man of power who fails to match his lover's
strength, Owen does not betray his Hester. He dies heroically in a
violent shoot-out and enters the realm of myth.

Wheelwright praises Hester as a survivor, and it is clear that, like
Frederick Busch, John Irving has committed himself to redefining
the role of women in the American novel even while he alludes to the
great male writers of the tradition. The bond between Wheelwright
and Owen Meany is as strong as those in the American novels that
have shaped the canon, and a territory beyond society is still attainable, even in the diminished domain of an attic. But the wilderness is
no longer a *masculine* wilderness. Encouraging women to step into the
wild, Irving shows that female presence does not threaten male
bonding but saves it. His narrator knows a central truth of America:
"We'll talk about Hester in our graves."

Larry Woiwode: *Born Brothers*

Much of Larry Woiwode's fiction reflects the heritage of his
family in the section of the United States bordered by North Dakota,
where he was born, and by Illinois, where he moved when he was
eight. He defines his novels about the Neumiller family as parts of a
larger cycle which he predicts will take five books to complete. As of
this writing, two of the novels have been published—*Beyond the Bedroom Wall* (1975) and *Born Brothers* (1988)—and each is a page in
what he calls a "family album." In an interview recorded in 1984
Woiwode describes his richest subject matter as "the people who are
pretty much gathered in *Beyond the Bedroom Wall*"; and he admits
that after his first novel, *What I'm Going to Do, I Think* (1969), he
needed to "get back to these people who are central to my life."[12]

A writer attracted to the relationship between autobiography and
memory, Woiwode points to a woman as the germ for the two novels
of the cycle published thus far, and he names Willa Cather and Co-
lette as the strongest influences on his work. Drafting a short story
about his grandmother, he began to sketch the frame for *Beyond the
Bedroom Wall*.[13] Conceding that the "center of the book" is Martin
Neumiller, he argues nevertheless that Alpha is "the emotional center, the pivot," because her death occurs in the middle of the tale.

He wanted, he explains, to show how "one must live" despite the loss of the mother. Deaths in the family and "the way generations influence and interact upon and with one another" are his primary concerns, and thus one understands his focus on the surviving sons and grandsons. In "Burial," for example, at the beginning of *Beyond the Bedroom Wall*, the elder Charles finally accepts the mandate to move on in life with "a certain amount of grace and power" after his father's death. Similarly, the younger Charles comes to terms with his own mortality at the conclusion of the novel even while he lives, whereas earlier his reaction to family tragedy suggests his evasiveness about the certainty of death. Since *Beyond the Bedroom Wall* and *Born Brothers* are, in effect, two long parts of an even longer story, I want to look briefly at "Burial" from the former before discussing the bond of brothers in the latter. A well-known proverb states that "a friend loveth at all times, and a brother is born for adversity." Taken from Proverbs 17:17, this biblical reference is the epigraph to *Born Brothers*. On the other hand, psychologist Mary D. Salter Ainsworth argues that even when kinship bonds are ambivalent, they are likely to be long lasting.[14] The tension between these two points of view is Woiwode's subject.

Woiwode's family album begins with the death of the patriarch and the long return home that burials require.[15] Deftly sketching the details with such unobtrusive descriptions as that of a man who is "a worse gossip than any number of women" (25), he suggests the attitudes toward gender that direct the North Dakota farming community where "Burial" takes place. The year is 1935, and that vast midwestern state represents one of the last territories for the man who would distance himself from society despite the presence of wife and family. The elder Charles would like to be that man. Although married, with nine children, he returns to bury his father as if he were a frontier scout on a mission, carrying only the necessities of straight razor and carpentry tools. But Woiwode knows that only the original patriarchs experienced the true wilderness, the land beyond the Red River that Natty Bumppo trod early in the nineteenth century and that Charles's father Otto first saw in 1881: "Trees were so scarce there was no lumber for building, and what sometimes looked like trees in the distance were the last remnants of the buffalo herds moving off toward the Missouri" (26). A sense of ending in more ways than one frames the finely tuned emotion of "Burial."

Today one would describe Otto as the kind of man "who built the country." No sexually pure Leatherstocking, he emigrated from Germany, married in Chicago, and prospered in North Dakota. When his wife dies, as women often do in American novels about the wilderness, his unmarried daughter exchanges the promise of her own life for the care of his, showing a "devotion to him [that] was always overabundant and colored with a childlike awe" (31). One cannot imagine Hester Prynne or Cora Munro stifling themselves with such readiness. This daughter will never leave the family homestead, cowed, as she has been, by such training in the proper role of females as "A lady must recognize a gentleman by bowing before he can acknowledge any acquaintance with her" (46).

That Otto wants to be buried on his farm, far from his wife's grave in the official cemetery, indicates the extremity of the separation of gender in the culture. The older generations of Neumillers love one another and care, but Woiwode does not sentimentalize their affection by idealizing the masculine-feminine roles that have shaped their lives. Just as Otto will be buried apart from his wife, so the elder Charles will leave his aging sister at the homestead when he moves to Illinois in search of the American dream. Not even in death are the traditional roles varied. Woiwode stresses the tenacity of male bonding when he shows Charles personally building the coffin, digging the grave, and preparing his father's corpse for burial. This is a bond not loosened but strengthened by death, even to the extent of reaffirming the son's faith in what he calls a just and caring God.

The death of the patriarch signals, however, the scattering of the tribe. In *Born Brothers*, Woiwode focuses on two siblings from a later generation of the Neumiller family who, because of blood ties, struggle to maintain their homosocial affinity in the face of displacement and loss.[16] Blond, quiet, healing Jerome works for thirty years to save dark, outspoken, unstable Charles, only to learn that the heart of the bond is the presence of pain. As Woiwode writes, "To remember is to admit loss and make ready for death" (6). The theme of "Burial" becomes the truth of *Born Brothers*.

What Charles remembers and Woiwode stresses is the competition at the center of bonding. Male aggression affects not only Other but self. Members of the family clan feel its lash as often as strangers from the alien tribe. Charles's earliest memory, for example, is of slapping away his brother's hand, and while Woiwode carefully avoids anything so transparently simple as a Cain and Abel theme, he knows nevertheless that males try to subdue each other whether they are brothers or not. Indeed, as a comparison of *Born Brothers* and *A Prayer for Owen Meany* confirms, the depth of the blood tie may increase the fervor of the subjugation. Like Natty and Chingachgook, and Ed Gentry and Lewis Medlock, Owen Meany and John Wheelwright forge their bonds outside the family circle and therefore may direct their energies toward those who would challenge them. Woiwode suggests, however, that literal brothers face a different trial. Bonded by birth and thus having no choice, they may find that despite genuine fraternity their energies are directed against themselves. Charles and Jerome love with a commitment foreign to Cain and Abel. The extent of their feeling governs the poignancy of their tale: "My brother. He was so much with me I didn't know who was who" (61).

Their wilderness is the impersonal big city—New York and Chicago—which cramps them both indoors and out. Accustomed to the space of North Dakota and the towns of Illinois, their trek into strange territory reverses the direction of Leatherstocking and his friends. As Charles admits about his hotel in New York, "From the day that I moved into this room, I felt threatened" (8). His pilgrimage, as he calls his journey to Broadway, brings him isolation tempered by nervous exhilaration, and the traditional Indians who speak strange languages and seem to watch his every move are Puerto Ricans, Slavs, and blacks. He acknowledges the foreignness of the metropolitan wilderness when he admits that the city "could as well be in Russia" (152). Separated from his bonded brother, Charles is a diminished Natty Bumppo without Chingachgook to guard his back. His defense is memory, especially of childhood with the mother, Alpha, and Jerome. Among his primary recollections is love for a mother who abhors the apparently natural aggression of young males: "Why can't she let us be American heroes, like the soldiers in the Saturday-night movies?" (66). Staring over his shoulder even as he hopes to find a future, Charles is caught in time, a sure sign that he will not achieve the status of the American literary hero who, as R. W. B. Lewis pointed out years ago, exists primarily in space. Time guarantees mortality in American literature, and early in *Born Brothers* one knows that Charles is bound for death.

Woiwode is very much aware of the anthropological thesis which argues that males must earn the privileges of bonding. This is why he shows that, even as a boy, Charles's urge to compete propels him from minor scrapes to serious accidents. Woiwode's commitment to realism ensures that Charles's misadventures are authentic for a male his age, but Woiwode also unobtrusively reminds the reader of the diminished myth now characteristic of the bond. Wanting to be like Gene Autry, for example, a watered-down, popularized re-creation of Leatherstocking, Charles is accused by his mother of acting like "wild Indians," the other side of the myth. Or, dressed in a skeleton costume for Halloween, he is paddled for playing the part too convincingly in front of a neighborhood girl. Such competitive rites of initiation backfire, for even as a child Charles must struggle to meet accepted requirements of maleness rather than merely engage in untoward behavior. One can imagine his chagrin when Alpha asks his brother to keep an eye on him. Only from the perspective of adulthood, while isolated without his companion in the jungle of the city, does he understand that "every fashion of attempted escape always ends in regret" (157). Male American novelists know this truth.

Alpha is the woman he carries with him into the wilderness, if only through memory. Unlike Busch, who keeps the mother on the periphery in *Sometimes I Live in the Country*, or Irving, who kills off the mother early in *A Prayer for Owen Meany*, Woiwode stresses her importance to the male psyche. To understand the unusualness of his position, one needs to remember the absence of the mother figure in such traditional novels of male bonding as *The Last of the Mohicans*, *Moby-Dick*, and *Adventures of Huckleberry Finn*. The matriarchal role as keeper of kitchen and culture is not a threat in *Born Brothers* as it is in canonical American fiction. Clearly agreeing with his narrator's sense of the female, Woiwode assigns Charles the key lines regarding gender in the novel: "Men should give their form to the family before they move into the world to form it in their own way, since they usually leave it to women to work out that form in everyday life" (101).

The failure of the male dream to secure the reality of life on the fantasy of myth drives Charles until his suicide. For he has learned early what the traditional American literary hero ignores in the need to confirm maleness: that not the father but the mother and grandmother "direct" the bonded males. Alpha is sensitive and thus vulnerable, a truth that first strikes Charles when he hears her curse in frustration. Although initially associated with Willa Cather's admirable women of the prairie, she is beaten down by the harsh life in the territory and the unpredictable heroics of her sons. Homage to the mother triggers competition in the brothers, as when Charles fails to please her on Mother's Day while Jerome succeeds. Charles's bids for her love—the boyhood accidents, the rowdiness, the sheer physicality of his presence at home—exacerbate her fear. He understands but cannot act on the lesson that male aggression alienates female love. Only the certainty of the male bond provides a measure of calmness. He overhears Alpha's verbalized sigh: "Here we thought we could keep an extra-close eye on him, having him along, and it turns out that he's even more unpredictable away from Jerome" (210).

The mother's decline accelerates when the Neumillers leave North Dakota for Illinois. Once a heroine of the prairie, as Cather, but not Cooper, characterizes women of the West, Alpha becomes a hermit in her new locale. Watching her, Charles realizes that she stares out the window to transform the weeds of her Illinois yard into the fields of the North Dakota farms. Woiwode's account of the central woman in the novel is an important modification for American fiction, for he refuses to accept the canonical paradigm that females flourish only in the settlement. Alice Munro (*The Last of the Mohicans*) and Esther Bush (*The Prairie*) are forced to return to the town where they supposedly prosper out of harm's way, but Alpha's life is over when she recrosses the border toward society. Woiwode shows that deterioration of the strong female has dire consequences for the bonded males. Through her authority Alpha has insisted that Charles and Jerome maintain their bond. When her influence gives way to fear, uncertainty infects their lives.

Woiwode's variation on the theme of male bonding is that his homosocial males long to save not each other but the female from injury and death. Her decline is a threat to their society of two. In *Born Brothers* the boys' need to help the mother is more than the natural love of children for parents because her death precipitates their pilgrimage. Fleeing the regularity of home for the adventure beyond the clearing, they must take the woman with them in memory. Male heroism is not defined by dismissing the female. Charles's lament is clear: "I wish I'd never wished that anything would happen to her so I could be a hero" (272). Unlike Cooper's Duncan Heyward with Alice, Woiwode's males do not have to find women in jeopardy to prove their manhood. Indeed, one could argue that heroism in *Born Brothers* is reserved for females. Alpha is the obvious example, but Charles's description of his wife illustrates his need for both women in the bond and their strength that he himself lacks:

> She drives our daughter to the pickup point for her early trip to school, picks her up again at night, cooks so many meals there's no need to mention the few times I stir up eggs. . . . She handles our accounts, shops, usually sees to washing the car and taking it in to be serviced, hauls home jugs of water from a well in a city park, . . . takes the children out for walks and to museums, carrying our son in a sort of sling affair across her front (284–85).

Woiwode's larger point reflects the position of Eve Sedgwick: that male rivalry for the female—first the mother, then the girlfriends of adolescence—helps rather than hinders the bond. Part of Charles's experience with Dewey, for example, is sexual initiation of course, but the more important element is that being with Dewey facilitates his first major effort to define himself outside Jerome's shadow. Unlike Leatherstocking or Lewis Medlock, Charles and Jerome run not from women but toward them, for the girlfriends also represent a psychological substitution of their love for Alpha. On his first date with Dewey, for instance, Charles fears that he has called her "Mom." Juxtaposing Charles's fumbling pursuit of girls with his admiration of the Western movies of Alan Ladd and John Wayne, Woiwode suggests that diminishment of the traditional American hero requires readjustment of the inherited attitudes toward gender. Charles longs both to be the hero—Joe Louis, Abraham Lincoln, John Wayne— and to keep the female by his side. Cora Munro would have been pleased: "Sometimes [Dewey] kisses me in broad daylight, which silences Jerome and his friends" (333).

But though drawn toward women, Charles is bonded to Jerome. The bond with the brother reaffirms the need for the mother. The tension is not strictly oedipal, for Alpha is dead. Rather, the point is that mutual love for the dominant female seals the commitment of the males. Woiwode's irony is that only following a serious automobile accident caused by Jerome does Charles gain even a semblance of Natty Bumppo's heroics. Drugged by morphine for his shattered legs, he remembers North Dakota and envisions "Indians, dancing and carrying bows." His longing for man-the-hunter heroism to impress the female persuades him to imagine the orthopedic pin that holds his hip and leg together as a "rod of arrowed metal" with barbs that protrude beneath the skin (381, 384). He should have been a pioneer with his great-grandfather Otto, but unlike James Dickey with Ed Gentry in *Deliverance*, Woiwode argues that mythic exploits have passed by the contemporary male. The only remaining territory is the asphalt jungle.

Of the authors discussed here, only Woiwode touches on the homoerotic overtones that might develop in male bonding, but the issue is always minor in *Born Brothers*. The loss of the mother and the compensating commitment to the brother cause Charles to seem vulnerable enough to be approached by a homosexual university classmate. Not sexuality but identity is Charles's dilemma, however, for Woiwode explores the psychological problem of fostering maleness away from the femininity that by contrast defines it. In *Born Brothers* gender opposition nurtures rather than antagonizes. This is why memory is the crucial force in the lives of the Neumiller males. Only by holding on to Alpha's fleeting presence is Charles able to rewrite the text of his life. With a sense of self shaped by how he remembers the mother and resembles the brother, he marries his wife because "the features of her entire face" are Jerome's (491): "there is no place I've been where Jerome hasn't appeared, through the door or an opening on memory" (508).

Woiwode acknowledges the legacy of the American literary tradition when Charles abruptly pulls up stakes to trek west back to North Dakota. In one sense he is in search of his past and thus foreign to the spirit of those who plunged into the territory to find the promise of the future. But in a more positive sense Charles hopes to step toward tomorrow by first rediscovering where he was. Unlike his mythic progenitors, he takes the female with him by equating femininity with the land: "If the land is like a woman, it's a woman no one can tame. 'And my spirit cannot be tamed by life,' I hear my mother say, in one of those echoes that arrive with greater force the further I move from her death, down the corridors of memory" (518). Charles lacks, however, his mother's spirit. Tamed by life to the point of drunkenness and instability, he finds himself, on his last return to North Dakota, alienated from the culture that once sustained him. Memory carries him only so far. Disputing his literary forebears, Woiwode insists that men without women are depleted in the wilderness. Charles finally understands that "the wedge of womanliness at my center is the tip of her heart that has passed into a cavity of me and now is beating out of control" (601). The bond that has always been necessary to his sense of self weakens when sundered from the woman who gave it definition. Fearing to live, needing to die, he directs his final thought to his bonded brother.

Ben Greer: *The Loss of Heaven*

Charles Neumiller's realization that not fathers but mothers and grandmothers "direct" both the family and the men within it is an interesting change in American novels written by white males. Matriarchal influence in American fiction about men is usually ignored (*The Last of the Mohicans*), subdued (*The Prairie*), or escaped from (*Adventures of Huckleberry Finn*). Even when the mother is an important character as in *The Sound and the Fury* (1929), a tale of destructive bonding among brothers, her authority is pernicious and justly criticized. One might point to *The Grapes of Wrath* (1939) with Ma Joad as an exception, but Steinbeck's novel details issues other than male bonding. Larry Woiwode's *Born Brothers* offers a modification typical of American literature of the 1980s. Ben Greer has similar concerns. Focusing on the grandmother figure in *The Loss of Heaven* (1988), Greer explores how she directs four brothers whose bonds extend into wildernesses as various as the rural South and Vietnam.[17]

It is significant that although a Southern woman, the matriarch in Greer's novel is not a Southern lady.[18] As powerful and wealthy as any aristocrat in *Gone with the Wind*, Harper Longstreet is not about to relegate her individuality to a code of manners or acquiesce to the inherited powers of patriarchy. In this sense Greer writes as much about the so-called New South as about newly defined concepts of gender. Despite the moments of melodrama in *The Loss of Heaven*, his method is effective, for he stresses the traditional adventures of the bonded males while detailing the untraditional authority of the single woman. Discovering matriarchal strength is not an issue for Greer as it is for Woiwode. Rather, Greer posits female authority at the very beginning of the novel and then follows the males as they grow up reacting to its influence. Orphaned young, the four brothers, for example, learn early not to indulge in socially sanctioned sentimentality about the old woman who takes them in: "I'm Harper. I'm not anybody's Grandmama or Gram or Nana. It's H-A-R-P-E-R to each and everyone of you" (4). Harper Longstreet is no grandmother of soft bosom and cookie jars. Tough, determined, and decisive, she clearly dismisses the notions of femininity by which she was raised as a girl earlier in the century. Greer sets *The Loss of Heaven* primarily in the 1960s and thus points to that tumultuous decade as the moment in American culture when restrictions on gender changed along with just about everything else.

Unlike Woiwode with Alpha Neumiller, Greer shows Harper Longstreet as not lamenting the aggression in male bonding but joining it. Where Woiwode emphasizes Alpha's femininity, Greer stresses Harper's androgyny, illustrating that inherited gender constructs are out of place in a society that altered as radically as the United States after 1963. One of Harper's first lessons to the males in her charge is, "You can't depend on someone else for the basics" (5). She means that people must figure out life by themselves, that neither she nor the brothers may play the role of Alice Munro waiting for Duncan Heyward and Leatherstocking to guide her through the territory. Bonded by blood and molded by a woman, the four males acknowledge her authority, either by reacting against or accepting it, as they step into the labyrinths of their adventures: one through a dark monastery as a priest, one through Asian jungles as a member of the Special Forces unit in Vietnam, one through the political quicksands of Washington as an adviser to President Johnson, and one through the night as a thief.

Since grandmothers are no longer sexual, Greer supplements Harper's matriarchal strength with a woman at the other end of the age spectrum. Fresh from a wilderness of her own in the coal mining region of North Carolina, Cat McGregor joins Harper to complete the female perspective that largely guides Greer's bonded males. Consciously placing *The Loss of Heaven* against the traditions of the canon, Greer characterizes McGregor's father as a latter-day Ishmael Bush—an anti-intellectual, vengeful patriarch who tyrannizes wife and clan. Greer then presents Cat as a daughter strong enough to repudiate masculine aggression. More important, he specifically calls attention to *Moby-Dick*, one of the pivotal novels of male bonding in American literature, when he describes Cat as first reading and then rejecting the standard premise of the tales that have defined American culture. Refusing to accept the wilderness in American fiction as a masculine domain, she reads Melville while "shivering in bed awaiting the arrival of the tattooed harpooner called Queequeg" (14). The privileges of bonding do not concern her; equality does.

Both issues interest Greer. *The Loss of Heaven* is a novel of male bonding, yet the bond is determined not only by a plunge into the territory but also by the presence of females who will not sacrifice themselves to the quest. Cat's muteness, caused by male aggression, is Greer's sign that dominance by the man denies language in the woman. Needing not merely a room but a word of her own, Cat will not speak until a vocabulary of accommodation rather than domination is offered. Greer clearly illustrates the dilemma. When Cat's father grabs the notebook she uses to express herself by writing, he equates the proper feminine role with silence: "Words is useless and anybody puts store in them is useless, too. Now get me my porridge" (19). One appreciates the irony when Cat escapes the father only to enter Harper's mansion where one of the brothers, resisting the grandmother, describes women as "your future dreamboat, your sugar, your main squeeze" (25).

Greer satirizes such insensitivity while characterizing Harper as the giver of wisdom and dispenser of gifts, the role normally played by men in the American novel. One example will suffice for the moment: the large tapestry that decorates a wall in the grandmother's house depicts a young Alexander the Great gazing from a mountaintop; the motto beneath the figure of the mythic male reads *Mundus tuus est* (The world is yours). In Greer's fictional world women claim an equal privilege. That Harper rules her newspaper company, her estates, her family, and her retainers like a refined and bathed Will Varner out of William Faulkner is not the issue. Similar to Cat Mc-Gregor with her Melville, the grandmother has been raised on Twain's and Kipling's novels of the masculine wilderness, and she has absorbed their perspectives on men and women. Greer's variation on the history of American education in gender roles is nicely formulated: rather than learn how to win friends and influence lovers, his women read the classics of male bonding and then apply the lessons to gain a parity denied women in the very novels they have just read. The words used to describe Harper suggest the androgynous nature necessary to affect the domain of male bonding that always surrounds her in the guise of the four brothers: "work and strive and control and dominate" (46). One hears echoes of "hard, isolate, stoic, and a killer."

Greer touches on the theme of androgyny—it is never a major premise of the novel—when he develops a modification of the Cinderella story for the first meeting between Harper and Cat. Inviting hundreds of guests to a costume party to celebrate her own birthday, the grandmother dresses appropriately as an elder Southern belle: black dress, high heels, jewelry. Cat, however, wears an aviator's uniform and is mistaken at first for a man. The irony is that the female belle plays Prince Charming to the male aviator's Cinderella, for wealthy Harper has the opportunity to conjure happiness for the backwoods Cat. Greer reverses the gender roles of the most famous fairy tale of male largesse and female submission. Even more important, he places their initial meeting in the grandmother's library, home of the language that Cat has yet to speak. Once again the young woman selects Melville as her talisman, "Bartleby the Scrivener," the definitive account of male stubbornness in American literature. As Cat goes to sleep in the castle of Harper's enormous estate, she writes eight words: adamant, trenchant, vociferous, harridan, optimistic, ebullient, sanguinary, and Pollyana (101). Taken together they describe the union of traditional masculine and feminine characteristics necessary to change a culture that encourages males to enter the territory while urging females to remain at home. Harper's concern illustrates Greer's point: "It's the last thing the world needs, one more giddy girl" (107). Confronted by Harper as to why she should not be returned to the North Carolina mountains, Cat rejects girlish giddiness and echoes Bartleby to speak her first words: "I . . . would . . . prefer . . . not to" (110). The scene is one of Greer's finest, testifying to his rewriting of gender requirements in the canonical American text.

Greer's characterization of Cat is not always consistent. Despite her repudiation of traditional male prerogatives, for instance, she longs to soothe Blackie, the most sexist of the Longstreet men. Unpredictable and untamed, Blackie steals jewelry from the rich for the fun of it, but his genteel lawlessness is more a masculine assertion against matriarchal authority than true criminality. Were Greer writing a century and a half earlier, he would send Blackie west of the Mississippi River with Leatherstocking. An author of the 1980s, however, Greer can offer Blackie only gloomy mansions and shadowed grounds as the territory beyond the grandmother's reach. Blackie's weakness is that he defines his relationship with the matriarch as if he were a fictional character in a nineteenth-century American novel: males must bend the rules of polite society that is always associated with women. While clearly sexual, Cat's desire for Blackie would seem initially to be Greer's concession to the outline of the traditional novel which generally shows women representing domesticity. But Greer skirts capitulation to this threadbare concept by casting not Cat but Harper as the dominant woman and main character in a novel that is largely about men. As one of the males says, "He and his brothers told Harper every detail of their lives" (163). Cat must earn a similar authority if she is to transcend girlishness. Her first lesson from the grandmother is the need of individual assertion: "If you get up early enough you can do anything in the world—anything at all" (165). One knows that Cat has learned well when, as a single parent, she dismisses marriage as "an institution that men use to suppress women" (336).

What Greer has done in *The Loss of Heaven* is develop a league of gentlemen molded by women. The occupations of his bonded males are disciplines historically dominated by men: the priesthood, the army, the government, and crime. These traditional bastions of male privilege have always offered refuge from the apparently tamer routines of female domesticity. But Greer's irony is the presence of the matriarch, and he means more than the old cliché that behind every successful man stands a good woman. Harper Longstreet stands behind no one. Indeed, she leads her men by pulling them after her, committed to avenging the weaknesses of patriarchy by shaping "good men, competent men" in her own image (219). Greer's most pointed revision of the biodeterminist thesis that males originally bonded away from the hearth because they were hunters is his account of Harper's father. A patriarch born with looks, intellect, land,

and capital, he squanders his heritage because he "just smiled and hunted and dreamed" (220). Witnessing the fallout from the male realm of hunting, Harper knows that eradicating the bond is not the solution. Rather, she turns the bonding process to her advantage, encourages a homosocial affinity among her men, and makes sure that she is the strength of the bond. Although she wears pearls to dinner, she is an accurate shot in the field. Cora Munro could have done the same had Cooper shown the imagination to complete her challenge to the gender relationships of her day. Harper's death does not end Greer's revision of the paradigm, for one suspects that Cat will take her place.

Greer deliberately characterizes one brother in the mold of the nineteenth-century hero. Proud of his Airborne and Ranger patches, Starkey takes his vision of the American wilderness to Vietnam. As one of the first military advisers in a territory far beyond recognizable borders, he accepts his role as a pathfinder and concedes that fighting in Southeast Asia recalls "the Wild West" (43). Like Natty Bumppo, he excels in the manly skills of the hunt, and he does not hesitate to kill when, in his mind, necessity dictates. Finally, he does not feel at all self-conscious wearing the uniform of a Confederate officer to Harper's party. He is a late-twentieth-century man with early-nineteenth-century standards of maleness, except for one major difference. Starkey accepts the equality of women and brings his most difficult decisions to Harper: "Sometimes he worried that he was dependent upon her and wondered if he could make a tough decision on his own, but he told himself that he had made a lot of solitary decisions and that it was foolish not to consult someone who understood him so well" (78). Greer underscores the significance of this revision in the concept of the dominant male when he establishes Starkey's bond with Blackie. Blackie rebels against the matriarch whereas Starkey adjusts. At the end of the novel the former is dead, while the latter is a hero.

Starkey's dangerous excursion through the Vietnam wilderness is a rewriting of Natty Bumppo's venture into Indian territory. Like Leatherstocking, Starkey is conscious that his white skin distinguishes him from the natives and marks him as the stranger. But he is no Leatherstocking regarding what Natty calls "the gentle ones." Although 12,000 miles from Harper, Starkey does not leave her behind. In a nicely understated scene Greer suggests that Eugénie, Starkey's mistress, is the younger side of Harper. Of French-Vietnamese extract, Eugénie is accustomed to "exotic privilege," large houses, willing servants, and social power. That her racial heritage differs from

Starkey's is the sign that Greer modifies rather than echoes *The Last of the Mohicans*. Unlike Natty, Starkey does not go on endlessly about maintaining his status as a "man without a cross." Loving Eugénie, he indirectly takes Harper with him into the wilderness, crossing the border from west to east when he hunts tigers instead of buffalo at Eugénie's plantation. When Greer juxtaposes Starkey's reading of Harper's letters with Eugénie's climbing into his bed in a house next to the jungle, one visualizes Natty Bumppo finally accepting the love of a Native American woman.

The satire of Lyndon Johnson's ignorance of Vietnam—"a chickenshit rice paddy. Hell, it ain't a war over there. I don't know what it is. But it ain't a war"—elevates Starkey by contrast to the level of American hero. Greer's Johnson is the ugly American, the man of power who indiscriminantly slaughters deer at his ranch and Vietnamese in the jungle, an Ishmael Bush with high-tech weapons. Starkey is bonded to male companions as firmly as Johnson, but he has Harper's photograph with him in Saigon. Johnson, in turn, makes fun of his wife. Thus Starkey feels sadness but not grief at Blackie's death and does not hesitate to reaffirm maleness by embracing war when Johnson begins sending in thousands of troops. Greer's joke on the misplaced American faith in Manifest Destiny and the subsequent need of a new frontier in Vietnam does not make Starkey laugh: "West. More Land" (270). Understanding him as shrewdly as Harper does, Eugénie defines Starkey as a nineteenth-century literary hero except for his acceptance of women: "You're bored with life. You want the sound of explosions and the rat-tat-tat of machine guns and the possibility of death" (275). Greer places him in the footsteps of Natty and Lewis Medlock when Starkey joins a tribe of Montagnards to hunt tigers as a prelude to killing the Cong. Hunting is hunting, be the prey animal or male, and Starkey realizes the primitiveness of this ancient test of bonding: "It was difficult to believe that in 1965, only a hundred and seventy miles from Saigon, in the middle of a modern war which made use of laser-guided bombs and computerized Gatling guns—it was hard to accept that men in loincloths were hunting man-eating tigers, but they were" (284).

Like American males from Cooper through Hemingway to Dickey, Starkey finds certain elements of war "beautiful and exotic and fun" (352). Greer does not shrink from the anthropological debate about the attractiveness of battle, the suggestion that as the ultimate hunt war is always possible because men always need to hunt: "Counting on your buddies in desperate situations, sweating with them, tying knots, breaking down guns with them and hacking through the green with them and finally going home at night and talking about it all around a fire and drinking booze with them— maybe this beautiful part of it was why there was war" (352). The implication is clear: male bonding causes war that is always fought by men. Harper consolidates her authority because she understands the premise of bonding. Starkey, in turn, keeps her with him metaphorically in the wilderness. Greer makes the point when he contrasts Starkey with a helicopter pilot who does not rely on women to moderate the bond: "Death. We do it bigger and better than anybody else. . . . Nobody can kill like a white, male, native-born American" (375). Sadly, D. H. Lawrence would agree.

Completing the association between Starkey and Leatherstocking in the description of the attack on the Viet Cong bridge, Greer gives Starkey two Montagnard companions armed with crossbows and sends him on a search and destroy mission every bit as harrowing as the rousing escapes in *The Last of the Mohicans*. Like Cooper's bad Indians, the Viet Cong represent Other, the alien clan to be hunted by Americans who would cleanse the wilderness of them. The issue, of course, is power, something that Natty Bumppo would understand, but it is not merely power against an always faceless enemy. Like Natty, Starkey wants the authority of command. As leaders of aggressive males, both equate strength with wisdom: "He loved the feeling of command, the feeling that his men were sleeping just beyond him, depending on him, trusting him" (405–06). Natty and Starkey will always take the first watch, be it Glenn's Falls or Vietnam. Their rites of maleness demand it.

The primary difference between them is that Leatherstocking must rid the territory of women as well as Iroquois, whereas Starkey wants women around him. His wilderness is no Eden, no green breast of a new land, and he himself is no pristine virgin playing at being Adam. Harper and Eugénie do not threaten his masculinity, nor does his pending marriage to Cat challenge his status as an American literary hero for the 1980s. For Greer, reality is more resonant than myth, especially a myth that speaks for an earlier era in the culture. Joining other white, American, male writers, he shows that the most significant recent social changes involve gender.

Richard Russo: *The Risk Pool*

The very name of the mythical town in Richard Russo's *The Risk Pool* (1988) confirms his awareness of the open space that has always engaged the imagination of male American novelists.[19] Located in upstate New York, in what might be called Cooper territory, Mohawk is named for the Native Americans who once represented Other to the bonded males who pushed them deeper into the forest. With his first novel, *Mohawk* (1986), Russo created the locale that he examines from a different angle in *The Risk Pool*, and, in the manner of William Faulkner with Yoknapatawpha, he follows many of the same characters as they meet grim circumstances with comic responses. Russo's Mohawk is a place of diminished myth, a dying town in which bonded men gather but which is unable to sustain the heritage of the Indian tribe that echoes in its history. As the narrator admits, "A great deal of territory had been surrendered since our ancestors had stolen the land and erected white churches with felled trees" (401).

Selecting for the epigraph a quotation from John Steinbeck's *Cannery Row* (1945), Russo nudges the reader to recall the bond among Doc, Mack, and the boys. Although he joins Steinbeck in describing his characters as saints or sinners depending on which "peephole" one peers through, he also uses the epigraph to remind the reader that bonding excludes females in *Cannery Row* and that women are useful to Doc and his buddies only for sex or memory. A marine biologist, Doc is an educated version of man-the-hunter who, like Natty Bumppo, is sensitive, intelligent, and courageous but who cannot take females with him into the field. The only woman who ventures beyond the border to the currents and eddies of the tide pools is caught on the rocks and dead. Similarly, with Mack and the boys' expedition to hunt frogs, a splendid, mock-heroic parody of companions on the trail, Steinbeck implies that female domesticity will ruin the home of "normal" men who prefer bird dogs and shotgun shells to white curtains and towel racks. For all his celebration of science in *Cannery Row*, Steinbeck remains a biodeterminist when portraying gender. This is not necessarily a flaw; his delightful novel was published decades before the insights of feminist anthropology. But his account of male–female relationships helps define *Cannery Row* as a fiction in the tradition of the canon.

Such is not the case in *The Risk Pool*. Russo's males share the experiences normally expected of American literary heroes, but their efforts to avoid women do not succeed. The primary bond here is between father and son, yet the bonding is originally delayed because the feisty mother has kept the boy from the wandering father. Thus Russo reverses the tension of Frederick Busch's *Sometimes I Live in the Country*, in which the father leaves the mother behind to enter the wilderness of upstate New York with the son. Mohawk is established as the outlying territory at the beginning of the novel, and the mother is already present. The question is whether she can stay there. Like Leatherstocking with Alice Munro, her husband would like to turn her back toward civilization. *The Risk Pool* begins with these words: "My father, unlike so many of the men he served with, knew just what he wanted to do when the war was over. He wanted to drink and whore and play the horses. 'He'll get tired of it,' my mother said confidently." But he does not get tired of it, and the mother learns that the father is celebrating not victory but life. Russo establishes immediately that Sam Hall sees himself as an American hero who equates life with activities that traditionally exclude women: "She could tag along if she felt like it, or not if she didn't, whichever suited her" (3). But following the birth of Ned—who narrates his own tale of initiation and growth—she files for divorce from the husband who is off playing poker the night she delivers the baby. What in different hands might have been material for a complete novel is for Russo a two-page exposition. In *The Risk Pool* he is more interested in the gender relationships after the separation of the male and female than in the melodramatics leading up to it.

Russo's irony is that the divorce is a long time coming. No Leatherstocking—though he would like to be with his big work boots and ready fists—Sam Hall needs Jenny with him—but not too close. From his point of view the privileges of male power teach that divorce proceedings must be initiated by the man. For a wife to do so would be to challenge the husband's manhood. Russo handles these domestic complexities with comic gusto as he shows how Sam's sense of identity depends on an understanding of traditional masculinity. Like countless American literary heroes who cry freedom when they feel hemmed in, Sam cannot reconcile the restraint of law and the promise of a free country. In his eyes, a "man certainly had the right to enter his own house and shout at his own wife, which was exactly what she'd keep being until *he* decided to divorce *her*" (9). That Jenny owns the house is not an issue with him. Unable to circumvent the law, and leery of his obligation to Ned, he disappears for six years and follows in the footsteps of his literary forebears when he runs away from the hearth.

The canonical novel in the background of *The Risk Pool* is *Adventures of Huckleberry Finn*, and thus when Sam returns to claim Ned, Russo alludes to Pap's attempt to entice Huck away from the company of women with the promise of freedom among a fraternity of men. Sam may be relatively honorable while Pap is always reprehensible, but both boys feel the lure of the masculine wilderness with their fathers as the pathfinder. It's the American way, as Russo knows, but Russo also understands that the position of women has changed since the day that Huck lit out for the territory. Huck's mother is conveniently absent, but Ned's is ready to challenge the traditional male prerogative. Jenny's comic yet earnest battle for the son is a fight that Sam does not expect. His masculine adventures in World War II fail to prepare him to contest a woman who thinks nothing of taking a stand. Russo shows that domestic battle lines are really gender issues: " 'This means war,' my mother said." The father replies, "Stay the hell home where you belong" (14, 15). Like Pap a century earlier, Sam asserts his power, breaks the rules, and kidnaps the boy.

Russo's intertextual re-creation of *Huckleberry Finn* also stresses the bond of white man and black man, but in *The Risk Pool* the affinity is between the father and his black companion Wussy. Though a boy, Ned must earn their acceptance by validating his maleness through such rites of passage as camping out and fishing. Like Twain's Jim, Wussy becomes Ned's spiritual guide through the territory, which for Russo is a deep-woods cabin beside a river: "I had caught fish and peed in the woods and not complained about my poison ivy. I had felt proud and important and good" (31). As Wussy explains, Sam Hall is such a "rockhead" that "your mother don't want nothing to do with him" (21). But unlike Twain, Russo does not mythologize the young man's break with civilization. Eating chili and onions before sleeping in a cold cabin is one thing, but having poison ivy and wet shoes is quite another: "I was scared enough to head back to shore on a squishy sneaker, aware that if my mother had been there, she'd have thrown a fit about my getting it wet" (24–25). What Twain and Sam Hall would like to define as the woman's domain is not so easily escaped. The line of demarcation between male and female space that once was stressed by novelists and sanctioned by culture is indeterminate in the 1980s. Jenny may not literally be in the big woods with Sam, Wussy, and Ned, but the point is that she does not need to be. Russo emphasizes that unlike Leatherstocking and Huck, his males will eventually have to turn back toward society, which in *The Risk Pool* is tempered by both the wildness of Mohawk and the independence of women. Jenny does not hesitate, for example, to fire five shots into Sam's car when the father returns the son to the mother. For Russo violence is not a characteristic biologically limited to men.

The Risk Pool suggests a different pattern for the need of American males to cross the clearing toward the wilderness. Rather than move steadily away from society as Huck Finn and Natty Bumppo hope to do, Sam creates a rhythm of leaving and returning. After Jenny shoots his car, for instance, he decides to "head out west and work on the interstates" (37). Yet he will always reappear in Mohawk for two reasons. The first is an irony that Russo and the reader but not Sam recognize: working on the interstates opens the trail to the civilization that Sam tries to avoid, and thereby shrinks the frontier even more. The second reason is that Sam is no virginal American Adam. Refusing to equate females with the Fall, he actively searches out the women who await him in Mohawk. Russo's rewriting of the traditional American text is noteworthy here, for rather than have the male force the female from the wilderness, he characterizes the woman as banishing the man from the hearth. In a manner that D. H. Lawrence probably would not expect, Jenny uses a gun to make her point. Besides, she reasons, Mohawk is in the territory anyway.

Given her rejection of gender restrictions, Jenny has no difficulty invading another citadel of masculine privilege, the Roman Catholic Church. There, amid altar boys, priests, and gardeners, Ned finds a male companionship that serves as a substitute for his bond with the father when Sam drives west. The only woman permitted in the rectory is the old cook, and Ned experiences a freedom that, if not as traditional as cabins in the woods, is nevertheless a boy's dream of camaraderie. He is not prepared, then, when Jenny plays Hester to a young priest's Dimmesdale. Rather than question her sexuality, as Hawthorne does with Hester or Cooper with Cora, Russo celebrates her repudiation of guilt. The morning after the priest spends the night with her, Jenny attends Mass, looking like "one of the stained glass windows, radiant and colorful in a summery dress. . . . She looked as radiant as the virgin who stood above her" (63, 66). When she takes Communion for the first time in years, one understands that Russo has modified the definition of the state of grace as well as indirectly queried the secondary status of women in the Church. For Russo the deception rests with not the female but the male: the priest betrays Jenny by sneaking out of town, moving west where American men traditionally run when they cannot face communal obligations.

Little wonder that Ned's first boyhood companionship is based on competition, a characteristic that biodeterminists define as unavoidably natural in males. But unlike Woiwode with Charles and Jerome, or even Twain with Huck and Tom Sawyer, Russo laughs at the urge that finds Ned and his friend Claude comically competing in everything from tossing beanbags to eating cookies. The cause,

Russo suggests, is not a biological imperative but a social form. Every time Jenny crosses the border to a male-dominated space, she is betrayed or repulsed. Untraditional assertion meets with traditional rejection, and Ned sporadically finds himself rebounding back into a masculine world. That Sam does not divorce Jenny indicates his need of women in a manner other than sexual, but his periodic absences deprive Ned of the balanced gender relationships that Russo shows are necessary to challenge the urge for male competition. As Sam tells Ned, "I'm not like your mother" (92). Even when Sam returns to Mohawk, the relation remains unbalanced because Sam takes Ned to live in places where he assumes women are not invited. The irony is that the woman is always present through her influence. One understands Russo's position that the men in *The Risk Pool* react to women rather than direct them.

All this is not to imply that Russo is casually anti-male. Sam Hall is a rough-and-tumble father figure who works hard whenever jobs are available, who gives reasoned advice to his son ("Don't grow up thinking you're tough"), and who shares his wages with whichever companion happens to be broke (103). That he breaks the law now and then affirms his kinship with literary rebels as various as Leatherstocking, Huck Finn, and Ed Gentry, and the bond that he feels for his son and Wussy is as old as American literature. Where he differs from his progenitors is his uneasy need of women. On the one hand, Sam sees himself as a typical American male suspicious of females outside the home. On the other hand, he admires women who crack the mold, who exhibit an androgynous strength in the face of social inequities. Russo does not shy away from suggesting that Jenny herself is part of the problem. Disappointed with Sam, she "dislikes the sort of men that congregated" in the places her husband takes her son: the Mohawk Grill, the cigar store, the pool hall, each a refuge for the male bond (118). Jenny lacks, in other words, the quality that Steinbeck praises in *Cannery Row*, the willingness to look through a different peephole. Ned is quite insistent on this issue: "I should point out that once I became known to the Mohawk Grill crowd, it was like having about two dozen more or less negligent fathers whose slender attentions and vague goodwill nevertheless added up" (119). Huck Finn was never so lucky.

Russo follows Ned's growth through adolescence, past the age of Huck, and thus to the moment when the attraction to girls rivals the bond with the father. Tria Ward is his Becky Thatcher, daughter of Mohawk's wealthiest family and, like Becky with Huck and Tom Sawyer, all but beyond his reach. Tria's and Ned's fathers illustrate a paradigm in American literature. Having fought together as young men in World War II, Sam Hall and Jack Ward nourish an affection for one another that is stretched but not broken by their unsettled lives in Mohawk. This is because Mohawk itself is at the edge of the clearing, hardly a center of society with all its attendant restrictions. Ned's admiration of Tria confirms Sam's companionship with Jack. Russo stresses the importance of their bonding: "Having awakened in the Hürtgen Forest remained a bond between the two men even now, something with the power to draw them together for five quick minutes in a dark bar for the swift exchange of secrets" (181). The secrets are for those initiated into maleness, a rite of passage that Ned survives in *The Risk Pool* without having to banish women to the settlement. Although committed to the masculine sanctuary of the Mohawk Grill, Ned admits that "life had taken a miraculous turn" when he meets Tria.

Part of the miracle is Ned's education about women. For his account of male initiation Russo establishes shooting pool, handicapping horses, and betting the numbers as the contemporary equivalents of shooting a rifle, hunting game, and tracking Indians. Sam teaches these manly skills to Ned as seriously as Natty Bumppo instructs Duncan Heyward or as Huck Finn helps Tom Sawyer, and in so doing the father eases the son's passage into the company of men. But that company is too restrictive for Ned. In a pivotal moment in *The Risk Pool*, Russo equates prowess at male competition with ignorance of female sensibility. The ceremonies of the canonical American novel will no longer do because women are no longer on the periphery of experience. Aware of the sexual metaphors connected with pool, Ned realizes in a manner that traditional American literary heroes rarely do that his crush on Tria changes his approach to the game: "But I never knew back then, nor do I know now, a real stud with a pool cue who could carry on a normal conversation with a woman" (216). The greater the skill with manly arts, the lesser the knowledge of female companions. Few male American writers are as unblinking as Russo on this issue: "The ignorance of such men concerning women is peculiar, many of them having participated greedily in numerous obscenities, and feeling no compunction about dropping their trousers in the dark room above the pool hall for some toothless old woman hired off the street at a flat hourly rate" (217). Russo's target here is not the casual player but the expert, the male who covers up sexual uncertainty with the bravado of power. In a passage worth quoting at length he illustrates how Ned's awareness of women is as significant to his growth as his acceptance by men:

I called Tria Ward just that once from the Mohawk Grill, and then I took up pool, a magic, hypnotic sport, a Freudian playground of balls, stiff rods, a variety of holes to approach from a variety of angles, all promissory, all destined to be filled, eventually, regardless of the shooters' skill. Don't take my word for it. Watch a foursome of thirteen-year-olds around a pool table in somebody's basement. . . . No thirteen-year-old sharpie is ever content to just sink a shot, he's got to ram it into the pocket manfully. . . . No thirteen-year-old but me, that is (217).

Caressing the cushion, easing the ball into the pocket, Ned learns how to value women without severing the male bond. This is an extraordinary moment in *The Risk Pool* and perhaps in contemporary fiction. Few heroes in traditional American literature accept even as adults the lesson that Russo's hero intuits as a boy.

The lesson is significant, for it enables the bonded male to live creatively with females in a way that Huck Finn would not understand. This is not to say that Ned ignores the outward arc from home that is a staple of American fiction. Not many years pass before he too joins "the great multitude of wandering Americans, so many of whom have a Mohawk in their past, the memory of which propels us we know not precisely where, so long as it's away" (264–65). But the lesson does mean that when Sam Hall leaves his fourteen-year-old son again, this time for ten years, Ned can pick up life at Jenny's with little difficulty. She may insist that the pool table and all that it signifies to her be kept in the garage, but her request is of no moment to a male who accepts the worth of both genders. Although his first reaction when Sam heads west again is to identify his father as a rerun of Huck's Pap, as the man by whom he "made dangerous friends and knew too damn much of the world for my own good," Ned realizes that Sam's conventional advice about hard knocks and survival serves him well. Ned does not, for instance, desert Jenny during her long recovery from a nervous breakdown, yet he continues to hone his skill at pool. Going west to college is both a natural act for him and, after living with his mother, a reassertion of the bond with the missing father.

Russo's account of the tie between the two men once Ned reaches adulthood is quietly developed. Sam's long slide toward final illness and death requires a shift in the proportions of the bond. For as Sam has more or less guided Ned through early adolescence, now the son must assume part of the burden of the father. As in most American novels, time curtails the male's escape in space. Sam must return to Mohawk when he is no longer young enough to survive in the territory. Russo uses Sam's reappearance to undercut the traditional complaint by a disappointed woman: "You men. How I envy you. The way you can just pack a suitcase when things go wrong" (349). In an America of diminished potential Russo knows better than to let Sam Hall join Natty Bumppo for a mythologized death at the far reaches of the West. Ned's lie to Jenny about his current work comically illustrates the point and reinforces Russo's sense of Mohawk as being at the edge of the clearing: "I was doing research in the concept of social hierarchy among primitive societies for my post-thesis in cultural anthropology. . . . The designation of Mohawk as a primitive society she accepted without hesitation" (310). That Russo's Mohawk is a long way from Cooper's Mohicans indicates the contemporary re-vision of the paradigm of the American novel.

Russo stresses Ned's position as the inheritor of a depleted past and the promise of a hopeful future when Ned edits a "stiff, awkward, dull, repetitious" *History of Mohawk County* (353). Written by Tria's grandfather ("Here's how the Iroquois stitched their moccasins"), the tome is such an outmoded narrative of America, such a canonical American novel as it were, that Ned attempts to rewrite it. His re-creation and his affair with Tria illustrate his need to include women in the story of the culture. Whether Ned will succeed in doing so is the question that he must face if he is to grow beyond Mohawk: "My father and Wussy were Mohawk men, which meant that somewhere along the line each had turned his back on a woman. Many had turned their back on more than one. Most now realized that in doing so they'd fucked up" (373). More insistent than other contemporary male writers about the fallacies of the men-in-groups syndrome, Russo treats with appropriate scorn the long-heard boast "that no matter how messed up we were, at least our lives were not being dictated by women" (373–74). One applauds Ned for joining in the scorn.

To complete his modification of the traditional American novel, Russo sends Ned away from Mohawk and toward Manhattan at the conclusion of *The Risk Pool*. Now middle-aged, Ned has learned what Sam resisted, that the possibility for a creative life rests within society and not beyond its borders. To follow the canonical hero is to die alone, as Huck's Pap do~s and as Sam Hall regrets at his own end. Leaving Mohawk for the last time, Ned finally rejects his father's example, repudiates the masculine wilderness of the American novel, and commits to a female just as one has hoped he would. For all his admiration of Sam's strength, energy, and imagination, Russo understands that the paradigmatic American hero has run out of both space and time.

Padgett Powell: *Edisto*

Simons Manigault, the twelve-year-old narrator of Padgett Powell's short novel *Edisto* (1984), understands from the beginning of his comic tale that the current changes in gender relationships have caused an immediate readjustment in his upbringing.[20] Like Ned Hall in *The Risk Pool*, he is left largely to his own devices; but unlike Ned, Simons relies on his mother as the guide through the wilderness. Powell's territory is Edisto, an island off the South Carolina coast and a place of adventure and freedom that Powell consciously contrasts with Hilton Head, the locale of civilization and decorum. Calling his mother "the Doctor" because she has a Ph.D. and teaches at a local college, Simons knows that conflicts based on gender have shaped both his character and his education. On the one hand, his father, who "cut out some time ago," instructs him in baseball, insists that he attend a college-prep academy for future lawyers and doctors, and urges him to read Jack London, one of the preeminent authors of traditional male privilege in American literature. On the other hand, his mother, whom the blacks nickname "the Duchess," disputes the father, sends Simons to a public school, and rejects the lessons of London. As Simons reports with a straight face that enhances the comedy of his colloquial speech, "They got in it over this, the one charged with sissifying and the other with brutalizing" (5). In *Edisto*, Powell refashions such culturally sanctioned stereotypes of gender as female gentility and male aggressiveness, and he writes a novel in which the woman is near the center of the young man's growth toward bonding. One understands the point when the mother—not the father—introduces the son as her protégé.

Like Richard Russo in *The Risk Pool*, Powell deliberately alludes to *Huckleberry Finn* to note the contrast between canonical American novels of male bonding and contemporary fictions that include women. Folk superstitions swirl around Edisto as they do the islands of the Mississippi River where Huck and Jim hide, and Simons does not hesitate to call the territory of his upbringing "a hoodoo coast" (8). More important, Powell celebrates Mrs. Manigault for not discouraging Simons's bond with the black man he calls Taurus. Thus the situation in *Edisto* is as old as American fiction: two males, often of different races, moving through a wilderness and away from a society that finds the dark-skinned man uncivilized and his light-skinned companion uncouth. Natty Bumppo, Ishmael, Huck, and Ike McCaslin have tramped Simons's hoodoo island before him, and they have bonded with Chingachgook, Queequeg, Jim, and Sam Fathers to avoid women in a society of two. But Powell varies the formula in at least two important ways. First, the female is permanently in the territory in the presence of the Doctor. Second, Taurus, who plays Jim to Simons's Huck, is as much Other to blacks as to whites: "He is shimmery as an islander's god and solid as a butcher. I consider him to be the thing that the Negroes are afraid of when they paint the doors and windows of their shacks purple or yellow" (8). The comic irony is that rather than be beyond the law (Chingachgook) or a fugitive from law (Jim), Taurus represents the law when the occasion suits him: he serves subpoenas.

One is not surprised, then, that Taurus accompanies Simons into the wilderness where the boy must validate his maleness by hunting. Powell parodies the anthropological hypothesis of man-the-hunter when he undercuts not the bonded males but the ritual itself. Walking with the female's blessing toward the island beach, "where the greatest natural resource is a toss-up between sand flea and mosquito," Simons warns Taurus to stand back while he "guns these things" (15). Using a long bugspray can "like a rifle," the boy passes the rites of initiation while the bonded guide nods approval. Leatherstocking shooting deer, Ishmael hunting whales, and Ike tracking the bear all belong to a different definition of the American novel. The Doctor knows this, of course—her academic discipline is literature—and thus rather than suspect the wandering male as a threat to harmony and home, she encourages the bonding as a means of easing her son's entry into experience. As Simons says of the primary independent woman in his life, "It isn't the first time she has solicited the attentions of your notably masculine types" (28). In Powell's comic re-creation of male bonding and initiation, the mysterious Other to be avoided is not Indians, blacks, or women but the Arabs who buy barrier islands and change them into resorts. Twain's Jim, himself forced to play the role of Arab, would recognize the problem.

In Powell's Edisto bonding is crosscultural. Arab millions may turn Hilton Head into glitz, but on Edisto, where even General Sherman never "got here to weed anything out" (34), pathfinders are still necessary. Taurus teaches Simons about boxing matches and beer, but Simons introduces Taurus to the black-owned club named Baby Grand. A native of the territory where Taurus is a stranger, preadolescent Simons is a local celebrity to both blacks and whites. He can walk into black "joints," order "tall-boy" Colt 45s, and escort Taurus to a pool table where "dudes" play while "sistahs" watch. But Powell stresses that the success of the bond depends on the power of the woman. Simons is permitted to wander through the wilderness because he is his mother's son: "The Duchess boy heah! . . . Ain't he somp'n" (8–9). This is a small but notable reversal in American literature written by white males, for in *Edisto* the bonded men rely on the strong woman for their identities. The reciprocity of bonding is significant, especially since it is between a white boy and a black man, but the more important cultural issue is the prestige of the woman who maintains her status in the hinterland without sacrificing sexuality or requiring masculine protection. As the narrator of his own tale, Simons sees himself as the hero, but Powell and the reader know who gives him his strength.

Encouraging Simons's role as witness, the Doctor nudges the boy in directions not normally available to the average adolescent. Powell uses Simons's observations for indirect political and cultural commentary much as Twain relies on Huck to expose social hypocrisies, but the significant difference is that Simons is aware while Huck is naïve. Where Huck must learn to recognize Jim's humanity, Simons accepts Taurus as a bonded brother from the beginning. Thus when the Doctor sends Simons and Taurus to a museum to look at tapes of an oral history program, she knows that both are shrewd enough social observers to spot the flaws. The targets here are sociologists and historians, academics who mistakenly think that they can film and explain a heritage even though they are from outside the culture. They do not understand, for example, such folk remedies as using sweet potatoes to cure corns and bunions, and as a consequence they represent the sound of the axes to Simons and his companions, the very civilization that Huck regrets and Natty deplores.

But though Powell joins canonical American novelists from Cooper to Dickey in using bonded males to describe the passing of an era, he differs from them by insisting that women do not cause the loss. Female sexuality, for example, is not a subject to be avoided but a reality to be explored. Powell gives Simons a natural curiosity about women that Twain denies Huck even though Powell applies a comic gloss to Simons's serious questions. In *Edisto*, however, the bonded companion rather than parents or teachers supplies the necessary information. One cannot imagine Natty and Chingachgook, Huck and Jim, or even Ed Gentry and Lewis Medlock discussing the complexities of sex and the value of women. To do so would be to undermine the prerogative that novelists have historically assigned to men in the wilderness. But Taurus and Simons do not dodge the implication that discussion of sex means the presence of women. Not the males but the Doctor has staked out the territory, and they understand that they are there by her consent. Talking about sex, Simons remarks of his bond with Taurus: "We must have looked like a real couple of cards, an ace and a joker maybe, sitting there in a haint-painted shack on a whistling bluff on the nowhere coast of Edisto" (84). Earlier American novelists would not be pleased.

As in traditional American literature, the threat to the bond in *Edisto* is domesticity. The irony, however, is that the return of the absent father rather than the presence of the mother upsets the equilibrium established outside the home. A lawyer and thus a representative of society, Simons's father cannot understand the need of his wife and son to remain in the territory. Urging his son to read of traditional masculinity in London's novels is one thing, but the father still plans for Simons to attend law school. In other words, he wants Tom Sawyer rather than Huck Finn as his heir. But Powell knows that American culture has changed and that Taurus promises a more contemporary definition of maleness for a boy on the border between wilderness and home. As Simons leaves his house after the father's arrival, he describes Taurus in a manner that emphasizes the black man's affinity with American literary heroes of the past: "It was Taurus, with a fire lit up under a triangle-shaped coffeepot, like in a cowboy movie. It was just like the open range. He was stoking dead palmetto fronds in. You could smell the coffee" (116). The point is that despite challenges by some feminist anthropologists, male bonding is a cultural if not a biological fact; the difference in *Edisto* is that the bond does not exclude women. One remembers that not Simons's mother but his father fears the threat to domesticity posed by the friendship between a white boy and a black man.

This is why Powell uses the final movement of the novel to describe Simons and Taurus as they "ratify" their experience together (119). Ratification of the bond is necessary given the resistance of conventional society, for unlike canonical literary heroes Simons and Taurus have no place else to go—no prairie, no river, no big woods. Powell makes his point by placing them on an island at the edge of the Atlantic. Their afternoon of fishing both confirms the bond and suggests their distance from Huck and Jim and from the era when males could escape home by floating all the way down the Mississippi River. These men can only catch a few mullet and then head *toward* society where they continue their ratification by taking two women sailing in Charleston Harbor. With comic verve Powell indicates the inappropriateness of nineteenth-century solutions to late-twentieth-century gender issues when Taurus's girlfriend not only joins the males but also wears a revealing bathing suit with a whale "spouting white spume" on the front (134). The womanless worlds of the *Pequod* and the raft no longer apply.

"Bound allies suffer a falling-out and become political friends," muses Simons. "Then they won't fight for each other anymore" (147). To validate the bond is to avoid such a break, as when Simons and Taurus have photographs of themselves taken by a man who instructs Simons that "evathang changes." Like Huck, the change that Simons dreads is the reassertion of traditional domesticity, what Huck would call the urge to "sivilize." The conflict between the settlement and the wilderness is a constant in American literature, even in the novels of the 1980s that do not automatically consign the female to the home. Thus the news that his parents have reconciled merely reaffirms the contradictory forces that affect Simons, just as similar forces frustrated his literary forebears. On the one hand is obedience to the man he calls "the Progenitor"; on the other hand is loyalty to the bond. Reconciliation of his parents means moving from the territory of Edisto to the society of Hilton Head: "I'd heard enough. The good old days were on a respirator. A boarding school and landed gentry snot-nose college-prep buggers for Simons Manigault" (151). Powell's ironic dig at biodeterminists is that the father in *Edisto* controls the hearth. Far from being man-the-hunter, the Progenitor insists on the values of the parlor. All the mother can do is apologize for inadvertently contributing to the split in the bond. She is, as Simons and Powell understand in a play on gender, "a good soldier," equal to the adventures of Natty, Ishmael, and Huck (152).

Powell deliberately undercuts the nostalgia that has been associated with American fiction ever since novelists realized that the encroachment of society meant the retreat of the wilderness. One experiences a sense of loss, a diminishment of freedom for the bonded companions at the conclusion of novels as various as *The Last of the Mohicans, Adventures of Huckleberry Finn, Go Down, Moses,* and *Deliverance.* It is not only that the demands of time inhibit the hero in space but also that the limitations of the female threaten the potential of the male. Powell rejects the paradigm. As Simons realizes when he drops by the Baby Grand for the last time, his black friends do not want him to "embrace like Boy leaving the jungle for Civilization and stiff British lips. All that's about as uncouth if not unethical as I could get" (154). Taurus hopes to head west toward new territory, but Simons's retort illustrates a necessary change in the definition of American culture that contemporary novelists have finally accepted: "if there's one left" (157).

There isn't, of course, at least not in the historical sense, but rather than equate the shrinking of territory with the imminence of death as canonical writers do, Simons carries his sardonic observations and the lessons of the bond with him when he invades the sterile civilization of Hilton Head. Not yet thirteen, he reaffirms the irony of his literary relationship with Huck when he scorns a place that Huck would naïvely admire, a place where "miles become kilometers, shacks condominia, marsh marina, and I feel like one of those bullet-shaped birds in Audubon's drawer" (165). What saves him from being permanently stuffed is the mother. Toward the end of *Edisto*, Powell reiterates the importance of the female to the maturation of the male. Simons looks at Mrs. Manigault, calls her "Doctor, Duchess, Soldier, Mother," and salutes her for fostering his bond with Taurus. With her bourbon, sexuality, and air of command, she personifies an androgynous strength that will not be weakened by the contained life in the settlement. Simons's praise of her suggests that his removal from the wilderness does not necessarily mean a dilution of masculinity: "I realize now I sort of trusted her as the commander all along, the man in charge, like at Parris Island, where they say that even though what they do to you and ask you to do looks bad, if not insane, you won't get hurt if you do what they tell you" (172). One realizes at the end of *Edisto* that the Doctor's literary ancestor is Cora Munro.

Rather than submit to nostalgia, Simons learns from the female to seize the day. Although he accepts the modernity of his new life in a glitzy community, he completes his tale by describing himself with a word that is as old as Leatherstocking in American literature: *pioneer*.

Robert B. Parker: *A Catskill Eagle*

Late in Robert Parker's *A Catskill Eagle* (1985), the detective Spenser says to his companion, "There's a book by a guy named Leslie Fiedler. Claims guys like us are really repressing homoerotic impulses."[21] Parker, Spenser, and his friend know that the quip is ironic; but Fiedler, one of the major theorists of traditional American fiction, refers to the fact that the standard hard-boiled detective story has long been a bastion of male ingenuity and cunning. Begun in the 1920s by the writers associated with *Black Mask* magazine, and thus an original American art form, the hard-boiled tale was a reaction against the cerebral sophistication of sleuths as different as Edgar Allan Poe's Dupin and Arthur Conan Doyle's Sherlock Holmes.[22] These educated gentlemen confronted heartless criminals and horrendous crimes, but they were as much at home in the drawing room as in the morgue. Raymond Chandler, for example, once described them as "detectives of exquisite and impossible gentility."[23]

Black Mask and Dashiell Hammett changed all that. By the time Hammett published *Red Harvest* (1929) and *The Maltese Falcon* (1930), the upper-crust detective had become the private eye, the man who often works outside society for the good of the social contract, the man who knows the gutter. More important, the private eye is a loner, a violent male viewed with suspicion by those within the law and out, a male who cannot take the risk of a bond. Hammett revised Doyle's popular formula of the brilliant detective committed to his bonded retainer when, in the climax to *The Maltese Falcon*, Hammett's private eye, Sam Spade, explains his rationale for "sending over" the killer of his partner, Miles Archer. Spade rejects as sentimental the notion that he avenges Archer because of a bond between them. Not emotion or biology but business is the issue. The murderer does not do Spade a "damned bit of harm" by killing Archer, but "when a man's partner is killed he's supposed to do something about it. It doesn't make any difference what you thought of him. He was your partner and you're supposed to do something about it. . . . When one of your organization gets killed it's bad business to let the killer get away with it."[24] This is a long way from the conventional American friendship that persuades Huck to go to hell for Jim. At best Spade's code is integrity mixed with cynicism, and it illustrates his position as an isolated male caught between the crooks and a system of law that he does not trust in the first place. Most of all, his explanation reiterates his refusal to let a female interfere with his code, for Archer's murderer is a woman.

The secondary status of women is a staple of the hard-boiled detective novel. As women sully Natty Bumppo's American Eden, so women threaten Sam Spade's honor. As he tells Brigid O'Shaughnessy, whom he may or may not love but who has killed his partner, "Don't be too sure I'm as crooked as I'm supposed to be. That kind of reputation might be good business—bringing in high-priced jobs and making it easier to deal with the enemy" (195). Sex with Brigid is one thing, but permitting her to manipulate him is quite another. She has counted on his attraction to her physical charms, and he fears that to "play the sap" for her is to compromise his manhood. Insisting that the mean streets are a masculine wilderness, Spade delivers

Brigid to the police as decisively as Natty forces Alice Munro from the forest.

Raymond Chandler, the second giant of the hard-boiled detective novel, seems at first glance to question Spade's suspicion of women, but this is because Chandler associates Philip Marlowe with a chivalric knight where Hammett likens Spade to a blond Satan. Opening *The Big Sleep* (1939), for instance, one immediately finds a pristine hero walking through dirty alleyways: "There was a broad stained-glass panel showing a knight in dark armor rescuing a lady who was tied to a tree and didn't have any clothes on. . . . I stood there and thought that if I lived in the house, I would sooner or later have to climb up there and help him."[25] Help him he does, but always avoiding the female's inviting nakedness. While Spade easily has sex with his partner's wife and the crooks' moll before casting off both, Marlowe keeps to his role of chivalric hero. To embrace the female is to tarnish the male. Rebuffing the sexual advances of the Sternwood sisters, he defines his distrust of women at the heart of his code: "The first time we met I told you I was a detective. Get it through your lovely head. I work at it, lady. I don't play at it" (141). In the traditional hard-boiled detective novel women are at best frivolity and at worst distraction. The lone male who spends too much time in the bedroom runs the risk of being killed. It's safer to keep the woman on a pedestal. As crime writer Elmore Leonard remarks, "When I was a boy . . . the women wore white gloves, they never got dirty."[26] Given Leonard's own hard-boiled fiction and its separation of male and female, one did not expect him to cast a woman as the lead in *Killshot* (1989), especially a woman who learns that men are usually mean and always unreliable.

Leonard's variation is an anomaly, however, for the hard-boiled detective story generally reflects the American literary tradition: novels written by white males about male power in a masculine domain. Robert B. Parker, the preeminent hard-boiled detective writer since the 1970s, has simultaneously brought a needed modification to the formula and illustrated how the change in the paradigm that I am suggesting also affects popular fiction. Author of a Ph.D. dissertation on the three classic writers of the genre—Hammett, Chandler, and Ross Macdonald—and thus very much aware of the literary heritage of his own novels, Parker has altered detective fiction in two important ways. On the one hand, he has moved it even closer to canonical American literature by having his detective, Spenser, bond with another male, and thus he has rejected the stipulation that the hard-boiled investigator walks into danger by himself. On the other hand, he has modified the canon by including a woman in the bond. Asked about his contribution to the hard-boiled tradition, Parker responds, "Love. I write about love. . . . If I have changed the form, whatever that form quite is, I think it's because of the degree to which I use it as a vehicle to write about love, which certainly not many hard-boiled private detective writers do."[27]

Rather than use women as a commodity as Spade does, or treat them as defilers as Marlowe does, Parker's Spenser admires their independence and accepts their equality. In love with Susan Silverman, a psychologist, and bonded to Hawk, a black man, Spenser is as far from Sam Spade as Spade is from Sherlock Holmes. The notion of the detective as man-the-hunter still applies, but the aggressive males need the female with them in the wilderness of Parker's underworld. All that the woman must do is recognize the reciprocity of the male bond. Susan learns the lesson in *Promised Land* (1976), the fourth Spenser novel, when she meets Hawk for the first time. A Ph.D. who is not afraid to grab a beer bottle to help Spenser face down a hood in Hawk's employ, Susan proves her value when she steps toward the violence. Parker modifies the American tradition by refusing to let the males see the female as a threat. Rather than kill her, as Cooper does Cora, or expel her, as he does Alice, Parker merely shows her that the man she loves is not that different from the man to whom he bonds, no matter how hard she tries to differentiate them. When Susan argues that Spenser helps people while Hawk hurts them, Hawk replies, "Not right. Maybe he aiming to help. But he also like the work. You know? I mean he could be a social worker if he just want to help. I get nothing out of hurting people. Sometimes just happens that way. Just don't be so sure me and old Spenser are so damn different, Susan."[28] Susan wants to see Hawk as a sidekick, as Other, as Tonto, or even to turn him into Magua, but Parker revises what today is a cliché. Not only are Hawk and Spenser alike, but they are different from the canonical American literary hero as defined by D. H. Lawrence. Although hard and surely killers, they are neither isolate nor stoic. Susan's presence is the difference. With her Parker reimagines popular American fiction and suggests that just as women do not necessarily compromise the male bond, so the bond does not always threaten love.

Parker joins heterosexual love and homosocial bonding in his detective novels and thereby changes one of the most widely read forms of American literature. Like Frederick Busch, Richard Russo, and Padgett Powell, he writes about a black male and a white male as bonded equals, but he is more insistent than his contemporaries that the homosocial companions are two sides of the same personality.

Parker comments that "Hawk is, and the racial pun is intended, the dark side of Spenser. He is what Spenser might have been had he grown up black in a white culture." Yet Parker is also conscious of writing within the tradition of the American canon to the extent that his hero is usually outside society. Like Sam Spade, Natty Bumppo, and Huck, Spenser and Hawk have to struggle against both the law and the lawless: "If such a hero is non-white," writes Parker, "his poise will be more radically asocial, because his exclusion will be more complete. While Spenser is both in and out of the culture, Hawk displays no such uncertainty. His presence in the books provides me an opportunity to examine some aspects of the American Myth, and to comment, sometimes directly, sometimes obliquely, on racism."[29]

In Parker's variation of the canon the bonded companion *and* the woman teach rather than inhibit the hero. Consciously alluding to the literary tradition, Parker has Spenser study Samuel Eliot Morrison's *The Oxford History of the American People* and describes Spenser as familiar with fiction and poetry. Spenser is also a former boxer who tries to keep his faith in the purity of sports. In *Mortal Stakes* (1975), the third Spenser novel, Spenser is trapped between the "jock ethic" and the code of the professional. As I have written elsewhere, "The jock ethic is the idealistic system of behavior that drives most great athletes to honor both written and unwritten rules even if losing is the result. Spenser innocently hopes that the ethic still holds when he transfers it away from the sandlot to the tougher game of protecting the weak and not killing unless required. The code of the professional is harsher. It demands that a person ignore idealism and fall back on expediency to win the contest at any cost."[30] The former suggests the younger America of the canon, but the latter reflects the soiled society that Cooper originally foresaw and feared. Parker's innovation is that not the bonded companion but the woman teaches Spenser about the fallacy of applying the jock ethic to a fallen Eden. One female calls him a "goddamned adolescent child" and explains that a shoot-out with murderers is not a playground contest "where you little boys can prove how tough you are." More important, Susan disparagingly calls Spenser's sense of male honor "all that Hemingwayesque nonsense."[31] Ridiculing such time-honored precepts of the masculine wilderness as "grace under pressure," she repudiates writers who celebrate men without women.

Spenser learns her lesson well in *A Catskill Eagle*. Acknowledging the influence of the canon by quoting Melville's prophecy for Ahab, "not of woman born," and by selecting a passage from *Moby-Dick* for his epigraph—"And there is a Catskill eagle in some souls that can alike dive down into the blackest gorges, and soar out of them again and become invisible in the sunny spaces"—Parker nevertheless challenges the tradition in general and Dashiell Hammett in particular. Rather than join Sam Spade and avenge his partner merely because vengeance is good for business, Spenser risks his life to free his bonded companion and then takes Hawk with him to rescue the woman he loves but fears he has lost. Like Philip Marlowe, Spenser "works at it" instead of plays, but he does not believe that sexual commitment to the female soils his status as knight. *A Catskill Eagle* begins with a cry for help from Susan, and Spenser hurries to the unfamiliar territory of the West to assist a woman who has preceded him beyond the border. One should note in passing that the California attorney he consults about freeing Hawk from jail is female. That she cannot arrange bail is not a fault of gender but a fact of law. Accused of murder and assault, Hawk is, as the attorney says with a straight face, "apparently difficult to subdue" (4). More important, she is a confident woman instead of an outraged feminist. When Spenser calls her "Ms.," she responds with "Mrs.": "I work criminal law fifteen, sixteen hours a day. I'm already more liberated than I want to be" (6).

Spenser's plan to spring Hawk from the sheriff is a parody of one of Cooper's outlandish escapes: the disguise, the hidden weapon, the bluff. Spenser even plays on the captors' prejudices, as Natty would do if he were rescuing a Mohican from a Mingo: in front of the police Spenser calls Hawk "Rastus" so that Hawk can retort "white belly." Parker caps the in-jokes when he has one bonded male warn the other of "the big sleep" and when he describes a large revolver as "good for whale hunting" (19, 21). Despite the allusions, however, he refuses to let Spenser play the role of Marlowe saving the Sternwood sisters singlehandedly. Spenser understands that Susan has been sexually involved with another man and that she has first asked not Spenser but Hawk for advice. Thus when Spenser and Hawk set out together to track down the kidnapped Susan, they are revising a staple of the traditional hard-boiled detective novel that calls for a man alone with only his code to guide him. As Hawk says, "We can fix up anything" (32). The emphasis is on the *we*. Parker's bonded males go after Susan not only because she asks for help but also because they need her. They may joke about the bond in racial terms as Ishmael and Queequeg occasionally do—"gorgeous Afro-American stud in company of middle-aged honkie thug"—yet they are not afraid of women in the territory, not even a lesbian friend of whom they ask help.[32]

Those reading Parker for the first time might think that Susan is in *A Catskill Eagle* merely to be rescued by the dashing male. Alluding to the beginning of *The Big Sleep*, for example, when Marlowe examines the picture of the captured lady and her knight, Spenser mentions Sir Gawain as he and Hawk climb toward a house that is described as a castle. Parker's point, however, is that the chivalric lover and Marlowe save their women in order to return them to society. Their notion of gender relationships persuades them that males roam the hunting grounds while females tend the fire. Spenser and Hawk believe otherwise. Conscious of feminist issues, they accept Susan as an equal who has as much right to cross the border as they and who seeks their aid not as a dependent woman but as a partner in need. More than other hard-boiled detective writers, Parker brings social issues to the formula. Sexism, racism, and certain features of the canon are his targets in *A Catskill Eagle*. This is why such quips as "I was sitting with my legs folded like Indians sit in the movies, and I was developing a cramp" are more than one-liners (70). They illustrate Parker's questioning of an American literature that persists in designating nonwhites and females as Other. As Hawk says of Susan, "She make both of us human" (82).

Spenser discovers during his rush through the mountains of the West that he has inadvertently tried to control Susan. Biodeterminists would use the word *coerce* and link it to male aggression, and in this instance they would be correct. But Parker's postfeminist male is capable of change, of understanding that to save Susan is not to reassert control: "What I can do is see that she's free to choose" (107). The dilemma, however, is not always clear-cut. First, the woman needs to be rescued, but she may resent the man who does so. Second, the male will have to go further than sheer physical courage: "I'll rescue her from Costigan and she can then rescue herself from me" (109). Finally, Spenser sees that Susan would be better off saving herself from the kidnapper, and that the male definition of female freedom is too close to dependency. He and Hawk can help, but they must let her decide. Alluding to the earlier *Mortal Stakes* and to Robert Frost's poem "Two Tramps in Mud Time" from which he took that title, Parker creates a bonded male who learns that love and need are one.

This is why the attack on the wilderness lodge in the Cascade Mountains fails. Although Parker makes it as exciting as any chase and rescue scene in Cooper, he cannot let the assault succeed because to do so would be to turn Susan Silverman into Alice Munro waiting for Duncan Heyward to spirit her away. This is also why

Parker chooses a town in Connecticut named Pequod as the site of Hawk and Spenser's next encounter with the enemy. One understands his homage to Melville's novels of male bonding and unstinting courage, but one also knows that the world of the *Pequod* is passé. When Spenser and Hawk recruit Vietnamese refugees to fight against reactionary white Americans who believe in guns, profits, and "the American way"—in what one character calls "frontier radicalism"— they illustrate Parker's rejection of a literary tradition that defines Indians as bad guys. The Vietnamese campfires recall those of the Mohicans, but the cultural situation has changed: the bonded males treat the people of another race as partners instead of sidekicks.

Spenser's mistake all along has been to idealize Susan, to take a twentieth-century woman and place her on a nineteenth-century pedestal. Projecting his needs onto her, he has obscured her sense of self. Her affair with Costigan is as much a gesture of maturity as a means of rebellion. Acting out a general thesis of feminist anthropology, Susan chooses which of several powerful males she will accept rather than wait, as sociobiologists would have it, to be chosen. With this one point Parker revises the gender relationships that have long been at the heart of detective fiction. As Susan says, "I need to set some boundaries on myself" and not permit someone else to set them for her (272). One of the boundaries that she refuses is the equation of female and home. When she reenters the wilderness to help the bonded males track down the culprit, she shows how far Parker's heroine is from the women of Hammett and Chandler.

The final shoot-out in the territory of what Spenser calls "the great West" is a reprise of the conclusions of many Westerns and detective stories. Purposely anticlimatic because the identity of the villain has long been known, the wrap-up is more a vehicle for resolving plot than a means of revealing character. The primary difference in *A Catskill Eagle* is, of course, the active presence of the woman. Parker even has Spenser compare himself to a primate as he enters the labyrinth for the kill, but by this point in the novel allusions to biodeterminist anthropology are ironic. The males charge into action because the female chooses them to act. Detective fiction may never be the same.

E. L. Doctorow: *Billy Bathgate*

Anne Tyler has remarked that the plot of *Billy Bathgate* (1989) is as "tightly constructed" as that of *Huckleberry Finn*.[33] Although her observation is accurate, Doctorow's allusions more often recall Cooper than Twain. Doctorow himself describes the Dutch Schultz gang as tribal, as a representative of Other in American culture: "Those guys are very tribal, and they live off at the edge of civilization, just where it abuts death. And the extremity of that life to those of us in the safe center is what pulls us." Pulled most of all, remarks Doctorow in a memorable phrase, is Billy, who succumbs to "the attraction to the disreputable."[34]

Billy Bathgate suggests that most Americans share a similar pull, a kind of mythic calling away from the closed house to the open spaces where one may experience along with Billy what it is like to hold a loaded gun for the first time. Lawrence sensed the American attraction to violence many decades ago, and he would have agreed with Terrence Rafferty's comment that "Billy is as much a small boy's dream of adolescent freedom as a good citizen's dream of lawlessness."[35] In this sense the Doctorow of *Billy Bathgate* is like the Cooper of *The Last of the Mohicans* sitting in a sunny parlor but writing about a dark forest. Dutch Schultz is Magua gone to seed, a charismatic leader stripped of nobility but nevertheless fascinating to the American psyche as a killer with freedom. But while a tale of male bonding between Bathgate and Schultz in which a female plays a pivotal role, *Billy Bathgate* does not illustrate the change in the literary paradigm that I have argued in this chapter. Thus I want to conclude this section by discussing a novel of the 1980s that is written by a white male, that shows two men bonding as they plunge into the wilderness to escape the law of the settlement, but that has no interest in revising the place of women in American literature. The influence of the tradition is still intense. Not every significant recent novel of male bonding rejects the secondary status of the female when the men light out for the territory.

This is not to proclaim that *Billy Bathgate* is gender-insensitive— I have no wish to politicize matters more than I have—but it is to stress again, if only by contrast, the refreshing unusualness of the gender relationships in the other novels examined. *Billy Bathgate* begins with an extraordinary scene of violence that borders on the comic, a scene that immediately attracts the reader to the disreputable, and a scene in which a desirable woman is the price of exchange.[36] Street-wise Billy, a quick-witted, articulate adolescent from the Bronx tenements, is judged by Schultz to be "a capable boy capable of learning"; and in the opening scene Billy confirms that the glue of the bond is the attraction of power (3). Fatherless and therefore ripe for bonding, Billy realizes today that Dutch is a maniac, but during the shocking moment years earlier when he watches

Dutch bind his partner's feet in cement before heaving him into New York harbor, Billy feels nothing but awe. His admiration for what he calls the "rudeness of power" is all the more intense because Schultz makes "the girl" witness the killing (3).

"He made me his," says Billy of the bond that is formed when Dutch finds him capable, and thus the boy has no compunction about describing the grotesquely comic but finally frightening boat ride during which the gang leader parades his strength. Dressed in black tie and white silk scarf, Dutch Schultz is Lawrence's hard killer without the myth. Elegant trappings merely expose rough edges. Doctorow describes him as if he were Magua trying to sip tea in Duncan Heyward's drawing room. Schultz is man-the-hunter in the extreme, the dominant male who, when the occasion suits him, reduces the men around him to subservient females; as when, in Doctorow's splendid account, the condemned man takes the arm of a formally dressed thug and "like some princess at a ball . . . delicately, gingerly, placed one foot at a time in the laundry tub in front of him that was filled with wet cement" (9). Like the bonded companions of the canonical American novel, these men live in what Billy calls "the realm of high audacity" (11), but they have none of the mythic purity that characterizes literary heroes who thrive beyond the safety of the settlement.

Doctorow clearly alludes to sociobiology when describing Dutch's obsession with traditional male privilege. Schultz is a primate with a homburg on his head and a gun in his hand. As if he had read biodeterminist anthropology, the condemned-man-reduced-to-princess likens Dutch to a favorite species for anthropological investigation: "'Cause you're an ape, Dutch. Hunker down and scratch your ass, Dutch. Swing from a tree. Hoo hoo, Dutch. Hoo hoo" (14). Their dispute is territorial, and like primates observed by biodeterminists, one sign of their power is domination of the female. Doctorow structures the opening scene so that blonde, elegant, erotic Drew personifies the sign of Schultz's ascendance in the male tribe. Exerting his right to the female in front of the condemned man who once had her, Dutch shows at the very beginning of *Billy Bathgate* that women are little more than a commodity. Billy describes the defeated male with cement shoes as having "a swarthy Indian sort of face," and one is back in the world of *The Last of the Mohicans* where women are the price of exchange between warring tribes. As if to ratify his status among the primates, Billy uses the occasion of Dutch's mastery of Drew to recall the moment when he buys his first pistol and then has sex with a barely adolescent orphan to whom he gives a dollar. Feminist anthropology is not an issue in a novel where manhood is all.

Drew is no virginal Alice Munro, however, exchanging sex for marriage. A witness to her boyfriend's murder, she must now trade sex for life. Once Doctorow places Drew as Schultz's mistress and then maneuvers Billy to be Dutch's means of keeping her watched, he reaffirms the pattern that the other writers discussed in this chapter have worked to change. This may be because he sets the novel in the 1930s, before the latest women's movement, but one knows nevertheless that it is only a matter of time before the female becomes the cause of male rivalry rather than the glue of male bonding. That Drew's husband is homosexual illustrates the homoeroticism that lingers beneath the surface of *Billy Bathgate*. However indirectly, Doctorow suggests that by seizing Drew, Dutch asserts sexual authority over a powerful male as well as what he assumes is a defenseless female. But Billy learns that Drew uses sex as a defense, as when he describes her with all the sexism of a standard male fantasy. Standing nude in front of her husband and Billy while deciding what to wear, she exhibits "the practiced efficiency of the race of women dressing, from that assumption they had always made that a G-string was their armor in the world, and that it would do against wars, riots, famines, floods, droughts, and the flames of the arctic night" (45). If men insist on turning her into an erotic icon, she will use eroticism against them. The conventional separation of the sexes prevails in *Billy Bathgate*. Billy perfects his role as the apt apprentice when, as the novice in the gang, he dreams of impressing the adolescent orphan girl with his new status as resident punk to the extent that she enjoys what he is "doing to her."

Billy learns quickly that the flaunting of masculine power affects homosocial as well as heterosexual relationships. For all the reciprocity involved in a novice–mentor bond, Doctorow shows that Billy stays with the gang because he fears the leader. Schultz is a killer losing control, his empire in decline. Lashing out at other males who threaten his privilege or invade his territory, he shoots before he thinks. The contrary nature of the bond poses a dilemma for the man who would go his own way. On the one hand, the bond with Dutch gives Billy identity; on the other hand, the violence may end his life. Thus Doctorow argues for a paradox when aggression becomes the defining characteristic of the bond. Admiring Dutch but hating unpredictability, Billy realizes, "If I didn't have him where I could see

him, how could I get away if I didn't know when to run? Then and
there I knew I had to be back with the gang, it was my empower-
ment, my protection" (105). Men in groups are safer than men alone,
even when the group endangers the individual.

This is why Billy accompanies the gang when it leaves the city
for the territory. Like many novelists before him, Doctorow chooses
Cooper country, specifically Onondaga in upstate New York, to set
the contrast between the wilderness and the town. Doctorow's comic
touch conveys the sense of bewilderment that denizens of sidewalks
and subways feel when they enter the countryside. Faced, for example, with fields, pastures, hills, and green, one of the tough guys
mutters, "I don't know about this, what do you do when you wanna
go for a walk?" (115). Ishmael Bush reincarnated, Schultz and his
retainers are out of place when they cross the border to where they
are "like travelers in some dictator's foreign country" (124). A statue
of the Indian chief Onondaga stands in the town square, but it irri-
tates Dutch the way Hard Heart bothers Bush in *The Prairie*. More
significant, Schultz, like Ishmael Bush, disrupts the harmony of the
bond by taking a woman beyond the settlement. Unlike the other
writers discussed in this chapter, Doctorow illustrates Carolyn Heilbrun's thesis of the masculine wilderness of the American novel.
Drew is no more than valued goods in *Billy Bathgate* in general and in
Onondaga in particular, a sexual release for Schultz and a cause of
disruption for the men. She indulges in a "kind of primordial action," but because Billy concedes that he knows little about women,
he is unsure how much she continues to exchange sex for life. She
has, after all, witnessed her boyfriend's murder. As the wonderfully
bizarre accounting genius, Abbadabba Berman, tells Billy, Drew is
"an X," meaning that even a mathematics wizard cannot determine
her value. Women in *Billy Bathgate* are always strangers.

Berman's solution to the puzzle of female Otherness is a concise
masterpiece of male misunderstanding. Women can't be crazy, he
says, so long as they comb their hair (269–70). Dutch's bewilderment
is more extreme. He appreciates what he calls "the idea of women"
because they give him something to own: "I like that you can pick
them up like shells on the beach, they are all over the place." Yet he
also idealizes women as if the best of them were not sullied by the
dirt of the world: "I think you only fall for someone, what I mean is
the only time it's possible is when you're a kid, . . . when you don't
know the world is a whorehouse. You get the idea in your mind and
that's it. And for the rest of your life you're stuck on her" (262). In
Doctorow's re-creation of the historical Dutch Schultz, the dominant

male divides females into virgins and whores. The division is a standard dilemma in the traditional American novel, and thus one is not surprised that Billy finally likens Drew to an Eve in the wilderness who shatters the loyalty of the father-son bond. Alluding to the American Eden around Onondaga, a countryside that Cooper would recognize when Billy sees it as "this noplace of such great green presence," Doctorow describes Billy's first sexual encounter with Drew as if they were Edenic innocents emerging from the primeval slime: "We applied this cold mud to each other and then we walked like children into the sinking darkness of forest, hand in hand like fairy-tale children in deep and terrible trouble" (216–17). Though not children, they are surely in trouble. On the literal level, the virgin-whore Drew indirectly causes Dutch's death when she is spotted by a rival gang boss. On the metaphorical level, she makes Billy confront the fallacy of his innocence when she splits the bond between the violent mentor and his willing novice. Once Billy has sex with Drew, he is expelled from the garden, no matter that his presence there is bogus in the first place.

In Doctorow's reprise of the canonical novel, then, there are no pristine Natty Bumppos to guard the wilderness and no virginal Alice Munros to give birth to a nation. There is only Dutch Schultz, the murderous extreme of the mythic American male, a hard, stoic killer who is an intruder in the territory and an anachronism in the town. He prospers because he encourages those around him to indulge in a sense of belonging, a means to breaking out of the isolation of the self. When Billy speaks of "the harmonies of gang life" (186), he is not ironic because he understands that male comradeship offers order. To run with Schultz is to claim a father, but it is also to be a possession, to accept that "the Dutchman takes care of his own" (208). Doctorow deftly indicates the distance between the commitment to bonding that defines nineteenth-century literary companions and the obsession with ownership that drives Dutch. Schultz is Doctorow's parody of the patriarch, the man of power who truly believes that he is a generous dispenser of patronage. For all the constraints of the bond, Billy realizes even while he tries to break away that Dutch is the ultimate father figure in the family that Billy needs: "I felt love for every one of them, there was a kind of consistency to their behavior that made me feel grateful for their existence" (260).

But Doctorow suggests that order is illusory, a chimera as fleeting as the glue of the bond. Schultz's murder throws Billy into a "whole new wave of fatherlessness," into a radical disruption of continuity that promises isolation. In one of the crucial moments late in the novel Doctorow, a master of blending fact and fiction, equates the severing of the bond with the factitiousness of history: "They have gone so suddenly, as if there was no history of our life together in the gang, as if discourse is an illusion, and the sequence of this happened and then that happened and I said and he said was only Death's momentary incredulity, Death staying his hand a moment in incredulity of our arrogance, that we actually believed ourselves to consequentially exist" (303). To reassert continuity, no matter how fraudulent, is the reason Billy tells the tale. Narrative creates history as well as fiction. By giving language to Schultz's inarticulate violence, Billy hopes to escape the random fallout, the death-dealing moments that by their very spontaneity negate the sequence of cause and effect that Billy has sought in the bond. Doctorow takes Dutch's dying monologue—a historical fact recorded by a stenographer[37]— and has Billy turn it into dialogue in order to validate the basis of his own life. Dutch may die by "dispensing himself in utterance," but Billy will live by immersing himself in words, "as if all we are made of is words and when we die the soul of speech decants itself into the universe" (308). To write the tale is to reclaim the bond.

But even then Billy takes his revenge after a gang member tells him that "horses or women alone is bad enough" (213). His sexual romp with Drew confirms the homoerotic foundation of the homosocial bond that such theorists as Fiedler have long detected in the American canon. He feels no guilt about his use of Drew because in his eyes she "trails" no history. She creates each moment, he thinks, free of the burden of time that diminishes males. Doctorow adds his own twist to the tradition, however, when he suggests that the male longs not to possess his bonded brother but to punish him. By having sex with Drew, Billy confiscates a property valued by Dutch and thereby acts out an oedipal vengeance against his always ambivalent father. That Billy later saves Drew from the gang is not as important as her status as an expendable commodity in a masculine domain.

Billy's return to the city is Doctorow's imaginative account of what Duncan Heyward, Ishmael, or Huck Finn might have felt while their companions either remained in the territory or died there. One's sense impressions are rearranged after a sojourn in the wilderness, and the settlement looks more crowded, as if it has been "worn out by history" (247). But for all his feelings of strangeness, Billy is at home on concrete instead of in meadows. True to the pattern of classic American fiction, Doctorow cleanses the wilderness of people who do not belong. Not many American writers detail the return of the bonded male. One admires Doctorow's understanding that Billy is suddenly too small for the territory but too big for the neighborhood. Experience changes character. Now a foreigner on his own street of tenements, he accepts the comic justice that New Jersey will represent all the strange land that he will ever have to know. Doctorow's final irony is that the dissolution of the male bond prompts the return to the female parlor. Billy ends up with his mother, an Old World immigrant, and his child by Drew, the New World Eve.

The pleasures of *Billy Bathgate* are extensive: the finely observed detail, the comic edge to the violence, the variety of character. The novel combines the historical aura of *Ragtime* (1975) and the nostalgic recollection of *World's Fair* (1985), and one comes away with the sense of an era caught. But *Billy Bathgate* is also what one may call a prefeminist novel, a distinguished fiction written by a white male that fits the paradigm of the canon. Doctorow's males bond, as they usually do in American literature, and his females are always the Outsider. The conventionality of *Billy Bathgate* points out once more the significance of the postfeminist variation brought to the canon by the other male writers examined in this chapter.

Notes

1. Frederick Busch, *Sometimes I Live in the Country* (Boston: Godine, 1986).

2. Mary D. Salter Ainsworth, "Attachments Beyond Infancy," *American Psychologist* 44 (April 1989) 712.

3. For a thorough discussion of *Rounds* and *Sometimes I Live in the Country*, see my *Domestic Particulars: The Novels of Frederick Busch* (Columbia: University of South Carolina Press, 1988).

4. Greiner 135.

5. John Irving, *A Prayer for Owen Meany* (New York: Morrow, 1989).

6. For a more complete discussion of these issues, see my *Adultery in the American Novel: Updike, James and Hawthorne* (Columbia: University of South Carolina Press, 1985).

7. "Doing Things His Way," *Time* 3 April 1989: 80.

8. "John Irving," *Book-of-the-Month Club News* April 1989: 2.

9. Irving himself lives part of the year in Toronto.

10. "Doing Things His Way" 80.

11. F. Scott Fitzgerald, *The Great Gatsby* (1925; New York: Scribner's, 1953) 121.

12. "Interview with Larry Woiwode," 1984, American Audio Prose Library, Columbia, MO. All comments by Woiwode are from this interview.

13. The story became a chapter in *Beyond the Bedroom Wall* titled "The Way You Do Her."

14. Ainsworth 715.

15. Larry Woiwode, *Beyond the Bedroom Wall* (New York: Farrar, Straus & Giroux, 1975).

16. Larry Woiwode, *Born Brothers* (New York: Farrar, Straus & Giroux, 1988).

17. Ben Greer, *The Loss of Heaven* (New York: Doubleday, 1988).

18. I use the term *matriarchy* in a general sense, though feminist anthropologists might disagree. See Paula Webster, "Matriarchy: A Vision of Power," *Toward an Anthropology of Women*, ed. Rayna R. Reiter (New York: Monthly Review Press, 1975) 141–56.

19. Richard Russo, *The Risk Pool* (New York: Random House, 1988).

20. Padgett Powell, *Edisto* (New York: Farrar, Straus & Giroux, 1984).

21. Robert B. Parker, *A Catskill Eagle* (1985; New York: Dell, 1986) 270.

22. For an overview of the hard-boiled novel, see George Grella, "Murder and the Mean Streets: The Hard-Boiled Detective Novel," *Contempora* March 1970: 14.

23. Quoted William F. Nolan, *Dashiell Hammett: A Casebook* (Santa Barbara: McNulty and Loftin, 1969) 22.

24. Dashiell Hammett, *The Maltese Falcon* (1930; New York: Vintage, 1964) 193.

25. Raymond Chandler, *The Big Sleep* (1939; New York: Ballantine, 1975) 1.

26. Mary Schmich, "Guns and Roses," *Vogue* May 1989: 220.

27. "Robert B. Parker: An Interview," *New Black Mask Quarterly* 1 (1985): 3–4.

28. Robert B. Parker, *Promised Land* (1976; New York: Dell, 1983) 88.

29. Robert B. Parker, "Commentary on *Promised Land*," *New Black Mask Quarterly* 1 (1985): 22.

30. Donald J. Greiner, "Robert B. Parker and the Jock of the Mean Streets," *Critique: Studies in Modern Fiction* 26 (Fall 1984): 37.

31. Robert B. Parker, *Mortal Stakes* (1975; New York: Dell, 1983) 142–43.

32. Parker writes about her extensively in the seventh Spenser novel, *Looking for Rachel Wallace* (New York: Delacorte, 1980), in which Susan and Rachel teach Spenser and Hawk about feminism.

33. Anne Tyler, "An American Boy in Gangland," *New York Times Book Review* 26 Feb. 1989: 1.

34. Michael Freitag, "The Attraction of the Disreputable," *New York Times Book Review* 26 Feb. 1989: 46.

35. Terrence Rafferty, "Worlds Apart," *The New Yorker* 27 March 1989: 112.

36. E. L. Doctorow, *Billy Bathgate* (New York: Random House, 1989).

37. William S. Burroughs once wrote a film script based on the police transcript of Schultz's final words: "The Last Words of Dutch Schultz."

Chapter Five

Coda:

Marianne Wiggins, Gloria Naylor, and the Issue of Female Bonding

Biodeterminists would have one believe that females do not bond. A reprise of a statement by Lionel Tiger illustrates their position: "In both violent and aggressive action male bonding is the predominant instrument of organization. Females tend to be excluded from aggressive organizations. . . . They do not form groups which are expressly devoted to violent activity or to potentially violent action."[1] I have already commented on anthropological evidence cited in feminist studies of primate and human behavior to question Tiger's claim. I should also like to point to contemporary literary evidence, and for this reason I conclude my commentary not by summarizing the earlier chapters but by proposing a coda. An examination of two novels published by American women in the 1980s, Marianne Wiggins's *John Dollar* (1989) and Gloria Naylor's *The Women of Brewster Place* (1982), suggests that females bond as readily as males. The coda illustrates that recent novels by women also contribute to the modification of the canonical paradigm argued throughout this study. Women bond in varying degrees in *John Dollar* and *The Women of Brewster Place* despite Tiger's assertion, but, unlike *A Prayer for Owen Meany* or *Born Brothers*, they do not rely on the opposite sex to secure the bond. The reasons may be political as well as anthropological.

I

The relationship between biodeterminist anthropology and contemporary fiction is as troublesome on the subject of female bonding as on the matter of man-the-hunter. In *The Woman That Never Evolved*, for example, Sarah Blaffer Hrdy confronts the issue directly.[2] A feminist sociobiologist—a term that many would deem an oxymoron—Hrdy disputes both feminists who believe that biological investigation is antifemale and biodeterminists who insist that the development of human society depended primarily on male bonding.

The reader may question such studies as Hrdy's that extrapolate conclusions about human potential from observations of primate behavior, but the point here is that Hrdy rejects Tiger's opinion that women do not bond. Indeed, she implies that the work of Tiger and other biodeterminists is obsolete. Based on her research in primatology she argues that females participate in such supposedly male activities as competition and bonding: "Selection favored females who were assertive, sexually active, or highly competitive, who adroitly manipulated male consorts, or who were as strongly motivated to gain high social status as they were to hold and carry babies" (14). One of Hrdy's significant conclusions is that female primates bond but that they do so "imperfectly" because they cooperate selfishly in an atmosphere of competition (100). Competition among females is well documented for every species of primate except the human, and Hrdy finds that not the absence of a competitive urge but the means of measuring it is the problem.

The tension between selfishness and cooperation in an environment of competition is a central concern in *John Dollar*.[3] Female bonding in Wiggins's novel is so fraught with violence and aggression as to make Tiger's comment questionable. Clearly indebted to *Lord of the Flies*, and frequently alluding to *Robinson Crusoe* and "The Rime of the Ancient Mariner" in order to heighten the atmosphere of savagery, *John Dollar* details the fate of a group of British schoolgirls left on an island without adult supervision after a tidal wave destroys the trappings of traditional authority. The novel may be read as both political commentary and religious parable because the girls are on the island for matters of empire and because allusions to the ritual of Holy Communion direct the climax. Wiggins reportedly considered titling the book *Eucharist*.[4] But my concern is with the matter of female bonding in a contemporary novel written by a woman about women and yet named for a man. For despite the importance of John Dollar as the exemplar of passion, knowledge, and ironic spirituality, the ostensible main character is a female. Young, "unsexed" Charlotte Lewes, a World War One widow, exchanges phallocentric discourse for what the narrator calls "Sudden Loss of Language" when she abandons dormant England for mysterious Rangoon. Dollar reawakens her to sex, an activity for which words are unnecessary, but Wiggins's primary interest in the gender relationships of *John Dollar* focuses on the bonded schoolgirls and the man they will devour during a celebration of the Eucharist.

Wiggins frames the complexities of bonding with the paradoxes of patriarchy. Apparently abandoned on "The Island of Our Outlawed Dreams" after paying homage to King George, the royal figure of fatherhood, the eight females believe that they must reestablish patriarchal order if they are to survive. Thus they write laws, rename objects, and honor authority; but these traditional staples of human society quickly disintegrate in the absence of male power. The girls' trek beyond the border to the territory of unknown vision forces them to bond in the aggressive manner that Hrdy affirms and Tiger denies, but Wiggins suggests that women-without-men is as sterile as its counterpart. Charlotte uses Dollar to reawaken into life. The girls literally feast on Dollar in order to live, but their ironic worship at a fleshly communion shrinks the bond. Wiggins's investigation of the relation between aggression and bonding says as much about Otherness as any novel by an American male.

John Dollar is a flashback, beginning with Charlotte's death as an old woman, but it soon turns to the island nightmare decades ago when she had "died before." Wiggins creates an air of endless menace as she details the bond between Charlotte and the younger woman called Monkey, who has cared for her from the time of the earlier "death." An Indian, an outsider, and an Other, Monkey is a female of a different race and thus the literary equivalent of Chingachgook, Queequeg, and Jim. Memory and silence form the center of her life with Charlotte: "They lost their religion to silence, they lost their forebearance to fear. Year after year they refused to forget, to look forward, look inward, look anywhere, but to sea" (5). Their experience with masculine power as illustrated in the arrogance of colonialism and the devotion to King George has made them leery of words. Most males as Wiggins characterizes them in *John Dollar* are devourers who make "one law for men, . . . one law for women" (7). Associating males with such verbs of consumption as *eats*, *chews*, and *buries*, she sets the foundation for an irony that becomes apparent only when the bonded schoolgirls feed on paralyzed John Dollar in a perversion of religious renewal. Erotic undertones and mystical obsession combine in Wiggins's dismantling of patriarchy. But not all males are a menace. Wiggins's irony turns on the realization that Dollar is a life-giver at different extremes for Charlotte and the girls, and that Charlotte kills the two females who destroy the sustaining male. In Wiggins's piercing description of gender, Charlotte is one of those "women who will try to cling on paper legs to the primeval" (10). She is a female who remembers love.

Love transforms Charlotte in the wilderness. No Alice Munro forever out of place when living "between known boundaries," she accepts unfamiliar Burma as a locale where England is only a myth, "a place more real in microcosm, in its re-creation, than in any actuality" (23, 21). Wiggins's strong female adapts to circumstances beyond the border. Rather than seek male protection, she repudiates patriarchy by rejecting conventional language. That is, Wiggins shows Charlotte reshaping her sense of self by reassembling words to signify objects in the territory that the English language cannot describe. She longs to live, writes Wiggins, outside "the King's Own Version of the text" (30). Her insistence on redefining life, objects, and language itself convinces the Burmese of her androgyny when they speak of her as "half-man, half-woman" (23). More important, Charlotte illustrates Hrdy's conclusions about females selecting male partners. Losing her husband in a war, the ultimate extension of male power, Charlotte surfaces from lassitude as soon as she chooses John Dollar for her lover. As if satirizing Cooper's obsession with blood lines, Wiggins shows her female pathfinder in the wilderness dismissing received notions of "the Empire's racial purity" when Charlotte takes Dollar despite his unknown origins. In Cooper parlance, she is eager to be a woman with a cross. Dollar's commitment to the discipline of reading reverses Charlotte's rejection of language, and thus Wiggins celebrates a creative bond that blends race and gender. Similar affiliations are either negated or neglected in the canonical American novel. One wonders, then, whether the inadvertent dissolution of their bond following the girls' dismantling of Dollar persuades Charlotte reluctantly to abandon her ideal attachment of male–female and withdraw to the silence of the female bond with brown-skinned Monkey.

Such dilemmas are not resolved in *John Dollar*. Wiggins resists the simple formulas of gender politics and explores instead the ambiguities of relationships when males and females, adults and children are swept ashore to a locale beyond law and tradition. One also suspects that Wiggins wrote *John Dollar* as the other side of *Lord of the Flies*, as a literary-anthropological protest to show that women do bond, that women are aggressive, and that such matters are not always felicitous for either males or females. Men exhibit colonialist presumptuousness while planning to rename the Island of Our Outlawed Dreams as King George's Island, and girls, like Golding's boys, collapse to violence once law is wasted in the wilderness of what the narrator calls "an alien and purposeless reality" (158). As Hrdy argues and Wiggins confirms, females bond "imperfectly" because they react selfishly when placed in an environment of competition. Charlotte is Wiggins's exception. Longing to be outside the King's text, she pursues experience that bears "a likeness to the fictions that one's dreamed" (69). Distortion of the fiction precipitates her lapse from language toward silence.

The irony is that the girls become their own menacing Indians once traditional language breaks down. Decorating their faces with paint and feathers, watching Komodo dragons slaughter spawning sea turtles, and finding a human skull that apparently has been partly eaten, the young women metamorphose into the alien tribes that American novelists have always pictured on the far side of the border. To conclude that "we have met the enemy and she is us" may be too neat, but Wiggins nevertheless suggests that the need to bond in dire circumstances and the perversion of the bond because of competitive violence are all but simultaneous impulses within each member of the group. She is much more skeptical than the male writers discussed in the previous chapter. Once the tidal wave propels the girls to the land of outlawed dreams where "no one was glad to discover that she was alive," they learn that their training to gather wood, construct houses, make fabric, mint money, invent wheels, name objects, and declaim laws is worthless (112). They believe that "to abjure the text" is to break the law, but, like Dickey, Wiggins places her bonded companions in a territory where the text is never read. Of the group, only Monkey, a modern-day Scheherazade with the texts of a hundred and one stories in her memory, survives.

With the girls' grotesque corruption of baptism, communion, and burial, Wiggins signals the final disintegration of the bond. John Dollar even compares the females to primates—chimpanzees—when he realizes that they have failed to organize their efforts at survival. They expect him to be God, the ultimate father, and tell them what to do. He expects them to be responsible human beings and make a concerted effort to live. Cannibalization of the male thwarts both expectations. John Dollar is no Natty Bumppo or Ed Gentry charging to the rescue to reassert the primacy of civilized male authority. Revising such assumptions of the traditional American novel, Wiggins describes the injured Dollar watching cannibals eat the girls' fathers—males killing males as in Cooper and Dickey—and then suffering a similar fate himself when two girls partially devour him in a perversion of the Eucharist—females killing males as in few other recent American fictions. Wiggins's final unexpected twist of the complex gender relationships in *John Dollar* occurs when Charlotte destroys the female bond by killing the two girls—females killing females as an illustration of the imperfect bonding noted by Hrdy. "Theirs," writes Wiggins in a disturbing understatement, "is failure of community" (189). In her intertextual nod to *Lord of the Flies*, bonds quickly disintegrate and the wilderness always wins. Normalities of gender are finally irrelevant in the domain of unknown vision.

II

Gloria Naylor is less skeptical than Marianne Wiggins about the durability of female bonding. Female solidarity is the subject of *The Women of Brewster Place*, so much so that no male in the novel has even the limited strength of John Dollar. Fathers, husbands, lovers, sons—all are either violent or absent, as they tend to be also in Alice Walker's *The Color Purple*. Naylor's men lead separate lives and do not bond. Usually patriarchal and always exploitive, they illustrate the dissolution of the black family because of the weakness of the black male. There is no Mr. O'Nolan (*Sometimes I Live in the Country*), Wussy (*The Risk Pool*), or Taurus (*Edisto*) to give sustenance, no Hawk (*A Catskill Eagle*) to lend individual strength. More important, there is no bonding in *The Women of Brewster Place* between black and white males. An unsympathetic reader might argue that O'Nolan, Wussy, Taurus, and Hawk are idealistic projections by white, male authors, updated but nevertheless nostalgic re-creations of Twain's Jim. Such skepticism does not concern Naylor in *The Women of Brewster Place*. Focusing on matriarchy, she writes about the widely perceived social phenomenon of the breakdown of the black family bond.

Feminist socioanthropologist Carol B. Stack disputes the phenomenon. A white scholar who conducted her research in a black urban community called The Flats where she lived for three years, Stack published her findings in *All Our Kin: Strategies for Survival in a Black Community*.[5] In her analysis of the prevailing cultural stereotypes of poor blacks, she challenges the conclusion that the "broken" black family unit, usually matriarchal, is "deviant." People within the group interpret their own circumstances differently from that of the norm. In Stack's words, they rely on "collective expectations and obligations created by cooperative networks of poverty-stricken kinsmen" that foster a stability usually ignored by outsiders (24). The point is that poverty facilitates bonding. The result is a necessary sharing of goods and services among those within the bond. Given such a framework of attachments, the traditional definition of the family (husband, wife, children) is inadequate to account for the support networks in a black community. Stack found that she had to redefine *family* as "the smallest, organized, durable network of kin and non-kin who interact daily, providing domestic needs of children and assuring their survival" (31).

Nevertheless, in discussing "personal kindreds," a kind of extended family involving kin and nonkin, Stack shows that the young adult black male often avoids the commitment traditionally associated with family responsibility. She describes Billy, a black woman with three children by three different fathers who accepts social as opposed to natural parenthood. Naylor uses literature to counter sociology and criticizes such evasion of accountability in her portrait of Cora Lee and the males who exploit her. Both contribute to the disintegration of family bonding among blacks. Stack, however, distinguishes between the folk system and the legal system of parenthood. The latter is the conventional definition of kinship and dependability; the former is "those people who actively accept responsibility toward" the children (46). These people are usually female—grandmothers of young pregnant black women, or aunts and sisters—and they assume the duty of raising the child. Thus the biological mother and the child's "mama" are not necessarily the same.

Fatherhood is a different issue: "Very few women in The Flats are married before they have given birth to one or more children" (50). The chain of socially recognized relatives that exists through the mother and her extended kin does not commonly apply to the father. Stack found that a child is accepted into the loose bonding relationships of the father only if the father becomes "an immediate sponsor of a child's kinship network" (50). She also learned that the community will tolerate the male's denial of paternity, though she argues that "the pattern whereby black children derive all their kin through females has been stereotyped and exaggerated in the literature on black families" (51). Naylor would surely disagree. Her characterizations of black males in *The Women of Brewster Place* are entirely negative. The result is her celebration of women and of the solidity of their bonds. From Stack's perspective the problem is environmental, because many black males lack the productive employment necessary to claim parental rights. If a male does little beyond acknowledging the child, he loses his rights: "The most important single factor which affects interpersonal relationships between men and women in The Flats is unemployment" (112). Stack's observation—devastating when fictionalized in *Brewster Place*—is that "mothers expect little from the father; they just hope that he will help out. But they do expect something from his kin, especially his mother and sisters." Activating these "kin lines" through exchanges and dependencies constitutes "the main activity of daily life for these women" (53). Clearly, female bonding is a potent force.

This social phenomenon is the center of Naylor's novel, but she takes a much less sanguine position than Stack on the problem of the absent male. Stack insists that the children have "constant and close contact" with men despite the "important role of the black female" (104). Naylor argues otherwise, though she would likely agree with Stack that, since women usually control the finances, men do not hesitate to cheat women economically. Indeed, the need to avoid exploitation may be the reason for the female bond. Stack quotes the reaction of an unmarried mother: "The point is a woman has to have her own pride. She can't let a man rule her" (110). The result is that many poor black females debase males to the extent of regarding them as inherently "bad" and thereby reverse the traditional association of women and the Fall. Faced with unstable male-female relationships, the females bond together because they realize that welfare checks and kinship networks offer greater financial security than the unreliable male. Marriage merely deflects resources from the female bond. Fathers are not always absent, as popular lore would have it, but they do lack authority. Stack's conclusion illustrates the strength of female bonding: "Kin regard any marriage as both a risk to the woman and her children and as a threat to the durability of the kin group" (117). Little wonder that she writes in her final chapter about "the domestic authority of women, and limitations on the role of the husband or male friend within a woman's kin network" (124).

Male limitations are unrelenting in *The Women of Brewster Place.*[6] Late in the novel the narrator describes a gang of black adolescent thugs as "the most dangerous species in existence—human males with an erection to validate" (170). The ultimate perversion of man-the-hunter, these males are a horrifying degeneration of bonding. Aware that they will never be called on "to thrust a bayonet into an Asian farmer, target a torpedo . . . or point a finger to move a nation," they cling together as a pack in order to hunt the one animal they can dominate: the female. Naylor's graphic account of their rape of the lesbian Lorraine is shattering not only because of the female's pain but also because the dazed Lorraine kills in turn the one male who has cared for her as a surrogate father. Lorraine's murder of the kind yet hapless Ben is a textbook case of victim killing victim, but Naylor rejects any suggestion that the marauding males are depraved because they are deprived. Stack argues that economic conditions compromise the identity of the black male. Naylor dismisses such generalities. In a scorching denial of male power, she blames the thugs themselves for their inability to exist outside the rat pack:

> They needed the others continually near to verify their existence.
> When they stood with their black skin, ninth-grade diplomas, and

fifty-word vocabularies . . . those other pairs of tight jeans, suede sneakers, and tinted sunglasses imaged nearby proved that they were alive. And if there was life, there could be dreams of that miracle that would one day propel them into the heaven populated by their gods— Shaft and Superfly (161).

Talking loudly, scratching their crotches, and calling each other *Man*, they feel threatened by any female who ignores what they assume is the power of their sexuality. As one of the males explains in an inadvertent play on gender, "Aw, Man, come on. Don't waste your time. . . . She ain't nothing but a woman" (162).

Sociobiologists might agree with his comment in terms of hunting, protecting, and evolution itself, but like the male novelists of the 1980s examined earlier, Naylor finds culture more complex than a domain of male prerogative. Her criticism of black men is as extensive as the biodeterminist undervaluing of women. *The Women of Brewster Place* illustrates Slocum's position on the primacy of the mother-child bond, Bleier's doubts about the importance of man-the-hunter theories, and Hrdy's evidence about female bonding. Yet Naylor goes further than arguing the equal importance of men and women. Her wilderness is the closed-off world of inner city tenements, but all males from the rural South to the urban North deserve secondary status in *Brewster Place*. Thus the epigraph to the novel— Langston Hughes's famous question, "What happens to a dream deferred?/ Does it dry up/ like a raisin in the sun?"—applies only to Naylor's bonded women. Similarly, Hughes's promise of violence in the wake of a dream forever delayed is relevant not to the raping males who have no dreams beyond Superfly but to the women who reaffirm their bond when they tear down the wall during the block party at the end of the novel. *The Women of Brewster Place* was written by a black novelist about black people, but gender is more important than race.

Naylor's men—always separate, never bonding—are variations of Mattie's girlhood lover, Butch Fuller. Attractive, fun, and unreliable where Mattie is attractive, serious, and determined, Butch personifies the emptiness that Naylor sees at the center of masculinity: "like puffed air and cotton candy" (14). When he abandons Mattie after getting her pregnant, he acts out the sociological phenomenon of the absent black father. Worse, he does not leave behind what Stack calls a "kinship network." One could argue that Mattie's father is a black man in the home, but when he thrashes his daughter for turning up pregnant, Naylor shows that he defines sexual independence in the female as a threat to the traditional power of the male. Mattie's son is no better. He also betrays her, but in this instance Naylor adds the complicating issue of female indulgence of male whim. Needing a man equal to her strength, Mattie spoils the boy rather than raises him: "She had carefully pruned his spirit to rest only in the enclaves of her will, and she had willed so little" (43). One could go on tracing Naylor's characterizations of the attorney, the minister, and old Ben the janitor, but her conclusions are consistent despite Stack's thesis to the contrary: the black family bond disintegrates because the men are either violent or missing. As another betrayed woman tells Mattie, "Let's face it. All the good men are either dead or waiting to be born" (61).

The Women of Brewster Place, then, reverses the traditional paradigm of American fiction and banishes the male from the female group. For the most part Naylor's women have many of the qualities that sociobiologists attribute to men. They are aggressive and protective, and they bond naturally. When society shuts them out, another woman takes them in. Male novelists from Cooper to Dickey illustrate R. W. B. Lewis's notion of the wilderness as the testing ground for the American Adam, but Naylor sees the archetypes of the Madonna and Eve. Her women bring not the threat of sexuality, as Cooper would have it, but the promise of nurturing. The woman who shelters Mattie and her son, for example, is named Miss Eva, and Naylor clearly identifies her as the source of female bonding. Human society develops from the solidarity of women, for they raise the progeny while the males wander the world alone: "In the unabashed fashion of the old, Miss Eva unfolded her own life and secret exploits to Mattie. . . . The young black woman and the old yellow woman sat in the kitchen for hours, blending their lives so that what lay behind one and ahead of the other became indistinguishable" (34). Where traditional male writers celebrate bonding primarily in the presence of aggression or during a confrontation with the unknown, Naylor suggests an unbroken attachment among women that stretches back to the Garden. Mattie is Naylor's new-world Eve, the inheritor of Miss Eva's wisdom and the dispenser of female strength. Another exploitive man may accuse a pregnant woman of being good for nothing but "babies and bills," but while holding the woman Mattie rocks her out of pain and into the bond that Naylor finds uninterrupted for all wronged females from Eve through Clytemnestra to the women of today:

> She rocked her over Aegean seas so clean they shone like crystal, so
> clear the fresh blood of sacrificed babies torn from their mothers' arms
> and given to Neptune could be seen like pink froth on the water. She

rocked her on and on, past Dachau, where soul-gutted Jewish mothers swept their children's entrails off laboratory floors. They flew past the spilled brains of Senegalese infants whose mothers had dashed them on the wooden sides of slave ships. And she rocked on (103).

The power of religious ritual traditionally limited to patriarchy—priest, minister, rabbi—is here assigned to Mattie when she washes the young woman clean of her agony and thereby baptizes her into the promise of the female bond.

Bonding among women weakens only in the presence of lesbianism. Naylor deftly suggests the uncertainty when the homosocial shades into the homoerotic, and she exposes women who deny one of their own. On the one hand, "the two," as the lesbians are called by the people of Brewster Place, try to live independently of men. They have no interest in the lovers and husbands of the local women. On the other hand, lesbian independence threatens the identity of women who define themselves according to approval by males. The lesbians' "friendly indifference to the men on the street was an insult to the women as a brazen flaunting of unnatural ways" (131). The continuum that Eve Kosofsky Sedgwick finds among female bonds, be they homosocial or homoerotic, does not hold in *The Women of Brewster Place*. For Naylor, the issue is not sexuality but self-sufficiency. The women on the block fear "the two" because the lesbians do not care for men. Females who are free of the cycle of weak males, violent domestic relationships, and unexpected pregnancy are denied the solace of bonding except among themselves. Lorraine's rape by the strutting adolescents who are no more than a parody of bonding is a physical male rendering of an unvoiced female resentment.

The block party at the conclusion of the novel that reasserts the female bond when the women gather to tear down a wall hardly compensates for the rejection of "the two." But it does illustrate what Naylor calls an "ebony phoenix," always female, always potent, often aggressive. Women bond imperfectly, observes Sarah Hrdy. In *The Women of Brewster Place*, Gloria Naylor shows that what matters is that they bond at all.

III

Comparison of the American novel of the 1980s as written by males and females is material for another book, one that I would welcome, but some preliminary observations may be appropriate here. In discussing new patterns in the historical development of American fiction that have not been identified before, I argue that representative male writers indirectly challenge the paradigm of the canonical American novel that posits two or more men bonding beyond the borders of civilization in order to avoid the inhibiting female. The female inhibits, so the males believe, because she represents society, restraint, mortality, and time. The novelists I discuss in the previous chapters are all white males, a conscious choice on my part because the traditional paradigm was originally established iń the nineteenth century by such white male writers as Cooper, Melville, and Twain, and extended for most of the twentieth century by Faulkner, Hemingway, and Dickey. In the latter decades of the twentieth century, however, many white male novelists have reexamined the paradigm.

In so doing, Frederick Busch, John Irving, and the other authors discussed here have not denied the enduring lure of the wilderness in contemporary American culture. Like their forerunners they identify the territory on the far side of the border as a realm of potentially limitless space, as a domain of freedom from restraint, as a promise of immortality. To reject the wilderness would be to dismiss a staple of American society, something these writers cannot do, as shown by their many allusions to the traditional novels of the canon. Yet they do question the long-honored stipulation that calls for avoidance of women as defilers of a virgin space. When the bonded males in Busch's novel, or Irving's, or Russo's cross the border, they find either that the woman has already preceded them or that they need to take her along. Rather than threaten the bond, women strengthen it, and they do so in such a persuasive manner that one sees the new American novel signaling different directions for American culture.

A general point about the directions is that they are not exclusive but inclusive. Both genders now enter a territory that was once the private domain of males. Such is not the case in the novels of female bonding examined in this coda. Female bonding has been inclusive in traditional American fiction. One thinks immediately of *Uncle Tom's Cabin*, but one also concedes that the women in Stowe's masterwork are generally not aggressive. For the most part their bonding is a matter of nurture, and Stowe's women of solidarity stand ready to embrace all who need solace. One notes with interest, then, both the sterility associated with female bonding in Wiggins's *John Dollar* and the violence in Naylor's *The Women of Brewster Place*. In these novels males are either destroyed or repudiated, just as females usually are in traditional American fiction. Thus one wonders whether a reversed paradigm is now in the offing *and* whether gender politics is the driving force behind the reversal.

There are many significant differences between *John Dollar* and *Brewster Place*, of course, but for my concerns a primary distinction is that Wiggins laments the elimination of the male in the presence of female bonding while Naylor insists on it. Although the former novel takes for its setting a historical moment nearly a century ago, and the latter is set on the margins of middle-class society, both are politically sensitive to the general upheaval in gender relationships that has changed most of America since 1980. *John Dollar* suggests that institutionalized male authority must be challenged, that nature itself will overthrow King George and his patriarchal representatives. Yet Wiggins also shows that individual males do not necessarily personify patriarchal dominance, that love between female and male is creative, and that aggressive female bonding can spin out of control, eventually cannibalizing reciprocal relationships. Females first devour the nurturing male in *John Dollar* and then destroy each other.

Women turn on women in *The Women of Brewster Place* also, but only when the lesbians are deemed deviant by the homosocial females who bond to protect themselves from men. Wiggins regrets the negation of creative bonding between individual women and men during aggressive consolidations of the female bond. Naylor regrets nothing of the sort.

Thus I conclude my analysis with a query that points to an irony: whether contemporary novels of female bonding written by women will reject the long-needed but now-realized alteration of the traditional paradigm established by canonical American fiction, an alteration that is urgently advocated in contemporary novels of male bonding written by men. Reading Marianne Wiggins and Gloria Naylor in conjunction with the writers discussed earlier, one wonders whether a new exclusivity regarding gender is to be formalized just at the moment when male authors have finally realized that women belong in the wilderness.

Notes

1. Lionel Tiger, *Men In Groups* (New York: Random House, 1969) 171–72.
2. Sarah Blaffer Hrdy, *The Woman That Never Evolved* (Cambridge: Harvard University Press, 1981).
3. Marianne Wiggins, *John Dollar* (New York: Harper & Row, 1989).
4. My information about the title may be found in Richard Gehr, "Sins of the Flesh Eaters: Marianne Wiggins's Carnal Knowledge," *Village Voice* 21 Mar. 1989: 50.
5. Carol B. Stack, *All Our Kin: Strategies for Survival in a Black Community* (New York: Harper & Row, 1974).
6. Gloria Naylor, *The Women of Brewster Place* (1982; New York: Penguin, 1985).

Sources

Ainsworth, Mary D. Salter. "Attachments Beyond Infancy." *American Psychologist* 44 (April 1989): 709–16.

Baym, Nina. "Melodramas of Beset Manhood: How Theories of American Fiction Exclude Women Authors." *The New Feminist Criticism: Essays on Women, Literature, and Theory*. Ed. Elaine Showalter. New York: Pantheon, 1985. 63–80.

Bleier, Ruth. "Myths of the Biological Inferiority of Women: An Exploration of the Sociology of Biological Research." *University of Michigan Papers in Women's Studies* 2 (1976): 40–41.

———. *Science and Gender: A Critique of Biology and Its Theories on Women*. New York: Pergamon, 1984.

Busch, Frederick. *Sometimes I Live in the Country*. Boston: Godine, 1986.

Carrigan, Tim, Bob Connell, and John Lee. "Hard and Heavy: Toward a New Sociology of Masculinity." *Beyond Patriarchy: Essays by Men on Pleasure, Power, and Change*. Ed. Michael Kaufman. New York: Oxford University Press, 1987: 139–92.

Chandler, Raymond. *The Big Sleep*. 1939; New York: Ballantine, 1975.

Chase, Richard. *The American Novel and Its Tradition*. Garden City, NY: Doubleday, 1957.

Cooper, James Fenimore. *The Last of the Mohicans*. Ed. James Franklin Beard, James A. Sappenfield, and E. N. Feltskog. Albany: State University of New York Press, 1983.

———. *The Prairie*. Ed. James P. Elliott. Albany: State University of New York Press, 1985.

Dickey, James. *Deliverance*. Boston: Houghton Mifflin, 1970.

Doctorow, E. L. *Billy Bathgate*. New York: Random House, 1989.

"Doing Things His Way" *Time* 3 April 1989: 80.

"Everyone's Notion of a Poet." *Time* 20 April 1970. 92.

Feidelson, Charles, Jr. *Symbolism and American Literature*. Chicago: University of Chicago Press, 1953.

Fiedler, Leslie. *Love and Death in the American Novel*. 1960; New York: Meridian, 1964.

Fitzgerald, F. Scott. *The Great Gatsby*. 1925; New York: Scribner's, 1953.

Freitag, Michael. "The Attraction of the Disreputable." *New York Times Book Review* 26 Feb. 1989: 46.

Gehr, Richard. "Sins of the Flesh Eaters: Marianne Wiggins's Carnal Knowledge." *Village Voice* 21 March 1989: 50.

Gelpi, Barbara Charlesworth. "The Politics of Androgyny." *Women's Studies* 2 (1974): 151–60.

Girard, René. *Deceit, Desire, and the Novel: Self and Other in Literary Structure*. Trans. Yvonne Freccero. Baltimore: Johns Hopkins University Press, 1972.

Greer, Ben. *The Loss of Heaven*. New York: Doubleday, 1988.

Greiner, Donald J. *Adultery in the American Novel: Updike, James and Hawthorne*. Columbia: University of South Carolina Press, 1985.

———. *Domestic Particulars: The Novels of Frederick Busch.* Columbia: University of South Carolina Press, 1988.

———. "Robert B. Parker and the Jock of the Mean Streets." *Critique: Studies in Modern Fiction* 26 (Fall 1984): 36–44.

Grella, George. "Murder and the Mean Streets: The Hard-Boiled Detective Novel." *Contempora* March 1970: 14.

Habegger, Alfred. *Gender, Fantasy, and Realism in American Literature.* New York: Columbia University Press, 1982.

Hammett, Dashiell. *The Maltese Falcon.* 1930; New York: Vintage, 1964.

Haraway, Donna J. "In the Beginning Was the Word: The Genesis of Biological Theory." *Signs* 6 (1984): 477.

Harris, Daniel A. "Androgyny: The Sexist Myth in Disguise." *Women's Studies* 2 (1974): 171–84.

Haskell, Mary. *From Reverence to Rape: The Treatment of Women in the Movies.* Baltimore: Penguin, 1974.

Hawkes, John. *Adventures in the Alaskan Skin Trade.* New York: Simon and Schuster, 1985.

Heilbrun, Carolyn. "Further Notes Toward a Recognition of Androgyny." *Women's Studies* 2 (1974): 143–49.

———. "Millet's Sexual Politics: A Year Later." *Aphra* 2 (Summer 1971): 40.

———. "The Masculine Wilderness of the American Novel." *Saturday Review* 29 Jan. 1972: 41–44.

Hrdy, Sarah Blaffer. *The Woman That Never Evolved.* Cambridge: Harvard University Press, 1981.

Irving, John. *A Prayer for Owen Meany.* New York: Morrow, 1989.

"John Irving." *Book-of-the-Month Club News* April 1989: 2.

Lamphere, Louise. "The Struggle to Reshape Our Thinking about Gender." *The Impact of Feminist Research in the Academy.* Ed. Christie Farnham. Bloomington: Indiana University Press, 1987. 11–33.

Lawrence, D. H. *Studies in Classic American Literature.* 1923; Garden City, NY: Doubleday, 1951.

Lewis, R. W. B. *The American Adam: Innocence, Tragedy, and Tradition in the Nineteenth Century.* Chicago: University of Chicago Press, 1955; Phoenix ed., 1958.

Lippert, Barbara. "Send in the Wimps." *Vogue* Nov. 1988: 414, 456.

Lowe, Marian. "Sociobiology and Sex Differences." *Signs* 4 (1978): 118–25.

Matthiessen, F. O. *American Renaissance: Art and Expression in the Age of Emerson and Whitman.* New York: Oxford University Press, 1941.

Melville, Herman. *Moby-Dick.* Evanston and Chicago: Northwestern University Press and The Newberry Library, 1988.

Naylor, Gloria. *The Women of Brewster Place.* 1982; New York: Penguin, 1985.

Nolan, William F. *Dashiell Hammett: A Casebook.* Santa Barbara: McNulty and Loftin, 1969.

Ortner, Sherry B. "Theory in Anthropology since the Sixties." *Comparative Studies in Society and History* 26 (Jan. 1984): 126–66.

Parker, Robert B. *A Catskill Eagle.* 1985; New York: Dell, 1986.

———. "Commentary on *Promised Land.*" *New Black Mask Quarterly* 1 (1985): 21–22.

———. *Looking for Rachel Wallace.* New York: Delacorte, 1980.

———. *Mortal Stakes.* 1975; New York: Dell, 1983.

———. *Promised Land.* 1976; New York: Dell, 1983.

Porte, Joel. *The Romance in America: Studies in Cooper, Poe, Hawthorne, Melville, and James.* Middletown, CT: Wesleyan University Press, 1969.

Powell, Padgett. *Edisto.* New York: Farrar, Straus and Giroux, 1984.

Rafferty, Terrence. "Worlds Apart." *The New Yorker* 27 March 1989: 112.

Reising, Russell J. *The Unusable Past: Theory and the Study of American Literature.* New York: Methuen, 1986.

"Robert B. Parker: An Interview." *New Black Mask Quarterly* 1 (1985): 3–4.

Robinson, Marilynne. *Housekeeping.* New York: Farrar, Straus and Giroux, 1981.
Rosenberg, Charles. "Sexuality, Class and Role in 19th-Century America." *The American Male.* Ed. Elizabeth Pleck and Joseph H. Pleck. Englewood Cliffs, NJ: Prentice-Hall, 1980. 219–54.
Rosser, Sue V. "Good Science: Can It Ever Be Gender Free?" *Women's Studies International Forum* 11 (1988): 13–19.
Rotundo, E. Anthony. "Learning about Manhood: Gender Ideals and the Middle-Class Family in Nineteenth-Century America." *Manliness and Morality: Middle-Class Masculinity in Britain and America 1800–1940.* Ed. J. A. Mangan and James Walvin. Manchester: Manchester University Press, 1987. 35–51.
Russo, Richard. *The Risk Pool.* New York: Random House, 1988.
Schifellite, Carmen. "Beyond Tarzan and Jane Genes: Toward a Critique of Biological Determinism." *Beyond Patriarchy.* Ed. Michael Kaufman. New York: Oxford University Press, 1987. 45–63.
Schmich, Mary, "Guns and Roses." *Vogue* May 1989: 220.
Schwenger, Peter. *Phallic Critiques: Masculinity and Twentieth-Century Literature.* London: Routledge and Kegan Paul, 1984.
Sedgwick, Eve Kosofsky. *Between Men: English Literature and Male Homosocial Desire.* New York: Columbia University Press, 1985.
Slocum, Sally. "Woman the Gatherer: Male Bias in Anthropology." *Toward an Anthropology of Women.* Ed. Rayna R. Reiter. New York: Monthly Review Press, 1975.
Stack, Carol B. *All Our Kin: Strategies for Survival in a Black Community.* New York: Harper and Row, 1974.
Tiger, Lionel. *Men in Groups.* New York: Random House, 1969.
———. and Robin Fox. *The Imperial Animal.* New York: Holt, Rinehart and Winston, 1971.
Trilling, Lionel. *The Liberal Imagination.* New York: Doubleday, 1950.
Tyler, Anne. "An American Boy in Gangland." *New York Times Book Review* 26 Feb. 1989: 1.
Webster, Paula. "Matriarchy: A Vision of Power." *Toward an Anthropology of Women.* Ed. Rayna R. Reiter. New York: Monthly Review Press, 1975. 141–56.
Wiggins, Marianne. *John Dollar.* New York: Harper and Row, 1989.
Wilson, Edward O. *On Human Nature.* Cambridge: Harvard University Press, 1978.
———. *Sociobiology: The New Synthesis.* Cambridge: Harvard University Press, 1975.
Woiwode, Larry. *Beyond the Bedroom Wall.* New York: Farrar, Straus and Giroux, 1975.
———. *Born Brothers.* New York: Farrar, Straus and Giroux, 1988.
Wylie, Alison, and Kathleen Okruhlik, Leslie Thielen-Wilson, and Sandra Morton. "Bibliography on Feminism and Science." *Women's Studies International Forum* 12 (1989): 379–88.
Zihlman, Adrienne, and Nancy Tanner. "Women in Evolution: Part I." *Signs* 1 (1976): 585–608.
———. "Women in Evolution: Part II." *Signs* 4 (1978): 4–20.

Index

This index does not include references to material in Notes and Sources.

135

9338